LIBERATION FROM
L O N E L I N E S S

Liberation FROM Loneliness

DAVID CLAERBAUT

Tyndale House
Publishers, Inc.
Wheaton, Illinois

First printing, March 1984
Library of Congress Catalog Card Number 83-51426
ISBN 0-8423-2157-8, paper
Copyright © 1984 by David Claerbaut
All rights reserved
Printed in the United States of America

For Ted

CONTENTS

1
LONELINESS TODAY

She can time it. Every night upon returning from work, as Mary unlocks the door to her dark apartment, it hits her: a rushing awareness of how lonely she feels. On Fridays, looking down the barrel at a weekend in social exile, it is especially acute. Monday morning with its return to the land of the living cannot come soon enough.

Many mornings Ed, a successful businessman, finds himself lying in bed thinking, "I don't really know who I am or where my life is going. I'm really in a fog."

It is painful for Marie to see how easily Jim falls asleep after a few loving words. If only she could pour out her heart to him. But he would never understand. In fact, he doesn't even really listen. He just isn't tuned in to her feelings or how to handle them. Jim is too practical and preoccupied with activities and projects.

Now that the moving is over and the family is settled, it sinks in. The old neighborhood is gone, the relatives are states away, and the church is a memory. This is a whole new environment. It is exciting but scary.

"There is an emptiness, a vacuum, right in the middle of my life," Bill blurts out to the minister. "Some nights I wake up feeling so

far away from God I'm absolutely terrified. I have everything I could want out of life, but I feel restless and anxious."

All of these people have one thing in common: though some are alone and others have the company of other people, each suffers from the most pervasive psychological malady of our time—loneliness. Each of these people is lonely in a different way. But they all are lonely. This is a book about loneliness—not just about what it is, what forms it takes, and where it comes from, but also about how to overcome it.* Loneliness *does* need to be overcome, for, like a silent enemy, it eats away at our emotional lives.

I hope that in the process of reading this book you will become less lonely—if only because I am writing it in a personal, from-me-to-you fashion. There is certainly no need for me to lecture at you or for you; that in itself is a lonely form of communication. Instead, I will be talking to you; and maybe, through taking notes and underlining, you will be talking back.

BASIC POINTS IN DEALING WITH LONELINESS

There are a few basic points we need to emphasize at the outset. First, as mentioned before, loneliness is common. Everyone experiences it. Yet, people rarely talk about it because, like death, it isn't chic. Admitting your loneliness is an act of vulnerability; it has a stigmatizing effect. Besides, often people don't like to be around someone who is lonely. Loneliness gives out negative, depressing vibes, and life has enough of those already. But don't be fooled. Loneliness is everywhere. Like death, it visits all of us, despite our frantic attempts to wish it away by not talking about it. It can't be avoided. But it *can* be overcome.

Furthermore, in the last analysis we are all truly alone.

---

*This is not a religious book. It does, however, contain religious material pertaining to loneliness.

We are born alone. We live our inner, thinking, and emotional lives alone; for example, no one on earth can possibly know even 1 percent of what travels through your brain or what emotional sensations you experience—no matter how receptive they might be or how skilled you are at communicating. In that sense, we are all strangers one to another. And, of course, we die alone.

Finally, being alone is not synonymous with being lonely. There have probably been many times when you have been alone because you chose to be. In those moments you felt nothing akin to pain or desertion. In fact, you felt at peace. You were able to commune with yourself and, perhaps, God. This type of being alone is so different from loneliness that, as you will see, it can actually help defeat loneliness.

Conversely, there have no doubt been times when you were in the company of others and felt lonely. They may even have been talking to you. But you felt isolated, apart, a depressing sense of emptiness. Instead of feeling nourished by their companionship, you sensed you were being served social junk food.

WHO IS LONELY

Loneliness can be defined as a feeling of desolation, being isolated, cut off, alienated, or estranged. It is the most frequently complained about (and I don't use the word "complain" in a negative sense) problem of our day. Any therapist will put loneliness at the top of the list of concerns his* clients express.

Loneliness is no respecter of persons. I work with lower, middle, and upper class students who suffer from it. I hold workshops for blacks and whites, males and females, professional and nonprofessional people who want help in handling loneliness.

---

*To avoid an unnecessarily clumsy his/her style throughout, the conventional masculine pronoun forms will be used. No chauvinism is intended.

To gain a sense of how universal loneliness is, consider that each of these people is lonely: the teenager who has just experienced his first unrequited love; the student, away at college for the first time (the explosive suicide rate among college students attests to their loneliness); the middle-aged person who feels something is missing in life and grows increasingly aware that his life span has an outer limit; the senior citizen, tossed on the shelf of society, waiting to die; the married person who has an amiable and superficially loving relationship with his spouse, while living in the dark chasm of emotional isolation; the parent, watching the last child leave the nest; the single parent, trapped in a child's world twenty-four hours a day; the newly divorced who lives, either with the guilt of having ruined a marriage, or the sense of rejection from being the one who was deserted; the widow(er), who feels a piece of her life is forever gone with the passing of her heart's companion; the never-married, who longs for intimacy and care; the attractive person whose life is filled with social contacts, none of which penetrates the emotional surface; the physically unattractive person who has no appeal to the Pepsi generation; the dependent who doesn't realize the smothering effect he has on the others to whom he so desperately clings; the businessperson with a high-voltage schedule, working amid ringing phones, conferences, and executive lunches—but who feels there is not a single person who cares that he is dying inside; the business or professional failure with whom no one wants to associate; the sick person who receives few visitors; the terminally ill whose company reminds others of their own mortality; the crusader who lives his values in a committed way—but alone; the pastor who hears the problems of his counselees and parishioners all day long but feels that no one could conceivably understand his own emotional wilderness; the black person, employed in an all-white setting filled with well-meaning people who cannot possibly know what it's like to be "the only one";

the affluent person with family, career, and friends, who is terrified at the thought of death—the ultimate loneliness—because he is estranged from his Creator; the Christian who works all day in a profane, agnostic environment, experiencing high levels of rejection and isolation.

Chances are, you too are lonely.

Like the child, sent to bed without supper, to ponder alone his misdeeds, everyone experiences loneliness. Not only is loneliness everywhere, but I suspect it is more common today than ever before. Why? Because there are a variety of social forces in today's society that intensify loneliness.

MODERNIZATION

Modernization and affluence have changed our life styles. Whereas our grandparents never tired of telling us how far they walked to school, how many hours a day they worked, or how exhausting their labors were, we live in an age of eight-hour days, air-conditioning, white-collar jobs, and automotive transportation.

As such, we have more leisure time on our hands—time that requires stimulation and preferably human contact to be enjoyable. Instead of working all day long, only to return home with a healthy feeling of exhaustion, we are faced with hours to fill—hours which, when not productive, produce guilt, regret, and of course, loneliness.

Modernization also brings with it higher expectations for "the good life." Survival is no longer the goal. Instead, satisfaction, fulfillment, and growth have become life objectives. We are bombarded with these heightened expectations. Best-sellers harp away at "fulfilling your potential," "being all you can be," "possibility thinking," and "living the self-actualized life." Human potential movements, from nationally advertised programs to special workshops at your local community center, suggest the possibility of a

Garden-of-Eden life available to those who seek it. It is easy to feel lonely when these expectations are not fulfilled, particularly when it appears that so many others are reaching theirs.

Moreover, we face an explosion of life alternatives. When your grandfather was eighteen, he probably knew what he would spend his life working at. His wife would certainly be a woman from the community. And your grandmother never thought to question her destined role as mother and homemaker.

Not so now. More than half of college freshmen will change their academic major at least once during their college career. To be twenty-two and without the vaguest notion of what career you will enter is not unusual. In fact, at forty people often change careers, start businesses, or expand their horizons.

The marriage bond is not always set in cement either— even among Christians. The quest for fulfillment some- times threatens faithfulness in a culture which seems to offer many more options than even a decade ago.

The effect of all these choices is to make it difficult to commit yourself to one coherent way of life. Yet it is through just such rooted commitments that clear, focused self-images are developed. Without a stable self-concept, you find yourself embarking on a long and lonely effort to discover and piece together the splinters of a fragmented sense of self. With all the uncertainty and alternatives today, many of us lack intimacy with our own selves as we search for a clear direction.

ROOTLESSNESS

For many, place of birth is not much more than a fact of biological origin. Once it was central. Where you were born was where you would spend your entire life. But with what sociologists call industrialization—the rise of cities, corporations, automation, and an educated, white-collar class—place of birth has little meaning. The odds are it is not where you are living now. With your parents living on an Iowa farm, your brother in the Sun Belt, your sister and her husband in the East, and you in another region, the roots of your heritage have been blunted. Once again, identity is threatened by a lack of depth and continuity. Loneliness sets in.

If you are married, your spouse may be the only one with whom you have a family tie. And she is likely someone you met after you became a young adult. Hence, relationships with earlier generations are absent, creating a sense of emotional suspension. The homestead of your youth exists mainly between the covers of your photo album. There is no sense of turf or tradition.

We live in the age of the nuclear family. With the average American family moving once every five years, your enduring contacts are few. The result of this mobility is to put a tremendous amount of pressure on your spouse, or perhaps a friend or two, to supply the emotional nurture and companionship necessary for healthy living. If the key figure(s) does not deliver the relational goods, the loss is felt more keenly. With no nearby brother or sister with whom to commiserate, or grandmother on whose shoulder to cry, the focus is narrowed and the expectations for the significant others in our life are intensified.

URBANIZATION

Urban living heightens feelings of loneliness. Urban life is characterized by radically increased numbers of human contacts, but encounters with little substance. Relationships in offices and bureaucracies are based on roles—occupational duties. It is no longer important how you feel or what kind of mental state you are in, only whether or not you can function on the job.

Impersonal relationships abound. Intimate, personal ones are at an ever-greater premium in this "what have you done for me lately?" society. Along with instant coffee and instant breakfast, we now have instant, but impersonal, relationships—all in the context of a changing society.

CHANGE AND STRESS

There is no single word that better characterizes our age than *change*. About all that is permanent in contemporary life is change. From *Future Shock* to cable TV, there is no escaping it. There are no emergency brakes to slam on.

With change come blurred identities, because the backgrounds—the frameworks—of our lives are constantly shifting. We are trying to see ourselves in moving mirrors. With nothing staid or in place, including our own personalities, we feel lonely—all by ourselves in a shuffle of activity.

Pressure mounts, demands increase, and the pace quickens, all adding up to increased stress. The effects of stress are legion and can be reviewed in any of a myriad of books and articles. But one of the consequences of this ferocious, modern-day anxiety animal is to drive people more inside themselves, to close them off. Thus they focus on coping internally with their ulcerated lives, rather than sharing their experiences unself-consciously.

OTHER FACTORS

Even TV produces loneliness. Mindless sitcoms and smiling faces in advertisements create an illusory world of people whose problems are few and whose lives are filled with excitement and stimulation. Moreover, after hours of this escapist brainwashing, we eventually press the "off" button, only to discover instantly that all those celluloid images were phony and we are alone.

Finally, with the widespread concern about loneliness today, there are those ever-increasing fads aimed at combatting the problem. Whether singles groups, health clubs, or noncredit self-improvement courses, they subtly or directly cash in on people's sense of social isolation. Unfortunately, they rarely work. When they don't, the victim is left more lonely than he was in the first place.

TYPES OF LONELINESS

Loneliness is not all of one kind. In fact, one can be lonely in one sense, but not in another. Below are brief descriptions of four types of loneliness. We will deal in detail with each in later chapters. Although there is an overlap among them, it is helpful to distinguish these various types to reduce some initial confusion over what you may be experiencing.

Social Loneliness is subdivided into loneliness within a relationship, called Loneliness In, and loneliness due to the absence of meaningful relationships, called Loneliness Out.

Loneliness In is particularly painful because here you are investing your energy in a relationship for the express purpose of experiencing genuine companionship of the soul, yet you are still lonely. The sense of deprivation and loneliness is heightened due to this "present but absent" paradox. Unfulfilling marriages, stormy romances, and erratic friendships exemplify Loneliness In. Loneliness In is very common, leaving a sense of frustration and anger since the victim innocently believed the myth that the solution to longstanding loneliness was simply being in a relationship.

Loneliness Out is virtually self-explanatory. Almost any sense of isolation, whether due to vacant love life or the absence of any intimate friends, typifies Loneliness Out.

Situational Loneliness is loneliness due to circumstance. It is temporary in that, if the situation is altered, the loneliness will disappear. Situational Loneliness commonly takes the form of Loneliness Out, but needs to be distinguished from it, because Loneliness Out can often be long term. Moving to a new neighborhood, changing jobs, going away to college, entering the army, or leaving on an extended business trip can bring Situational Loneliness.

Intrapsychic (within the self) *Loneliness* refers to a sense of alienation from self. Often this is due to lack of a clear and certain identity, of knowing who you are and where you are going. In an era of constant change, expanding life choices, and competing ideologies, making it difficult to know where or in what to invest your life, this type of loneliness is widespread.

A fuzzy sense of self makes it difficult ever to be at peace with yourself, to enjoy communing with yourself and being your own best friend. There is confusion, an uneasiness or restlessness inside as the search for a coherent self continues. College students who need to take a term off to "find themselves"; suburban housewives who feel their lives are getting away from them, due to isolation and identity diffusion; and men who live in the corporate express lane and have little time to find out who they really are—all suffer from Intrapsychic Loneliness.

Spiritual Loneliness is due to a separation of the person from God. Nonbelievers experience a great deal of this, sensing a vacuum of meaning at the core of their lives. Ruth Armstrong points to this, citing a study by Buhler in which she asked her subjects what was "ultimately important" to them. Most of them had no idea whatsoever.[1] In the case of the unbeliever, Spiritual Loneliness often spills over into Intrapsychic Loneliness due to this lack of inner peace.

Christians are by no means immune to Spiritual Loneliness either. Books on unanswered prayer, intimacy with God, and fillings of the Holy Spirit attest to the painful gaps in the lives of many Christians.

LONELINESS IN MASLOW'S HIERARCHY
To appreciate how basic loneliness is, it helps to review briefly a well-known psychological model with which you may be familiar. It is Abraham Maslow's Hierarchy of Needs (see Figure 1).[2]

According to Maslow, humans have five essential needs, each of which must be met—in order—if genuine mental health is to be experienced. His model is in the shape of a triangle because as one ascends the hierarchy, the needs become more difficult to meet.

At the base of the triangle is the physiological level. This is understandable, for if one's survival needs are not met, life itself will be snuffed out. In fact, if one is threatened at this level, absolutely nothing else will seem important. For instance, an otherwise civilized person might even kill over a glass of fresh water while stranded on a salt water ocean.

It is easy to dismiss the importance of this level because we have little firsthand experience with it. However, if anything, this should be cause for greater thankfulness, considering that about two-thirds of the world confronts this need level daily.

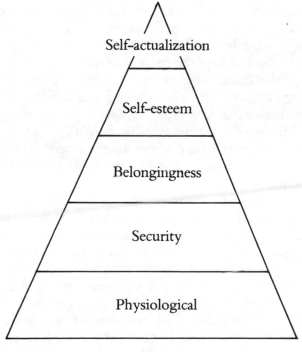

Figure 1
MASLOW'S HIERARCHY OF NEEDS

The second level, security, refers to having the survival needs met over an indefinite period—for the foreseeable future. If it looks as if your survival will be in jeopardy down the road, you most likely will pull out all the stops to secure it. Savings accounts, pensions, Individual Retirement Accounts, and insurance policies are the American way of dealing with the security level.

If the security needs are pretty well in place, a person then shifts to the belongingness level. Belongingness includes love and attention. Here is where relationships count. This is where Loneliness In and Loneliness Out are felt. As long as you are preoccupied with survival or security matters, relationships will be an afterthought. However, once belongingness emerges as a need, it becomes all-encompassing.

I remember one young man in his thirties, whose commissions alone in the commodities market averaged a quarter of a million dollars a year. He lost his marriage and spent most of his time trying to reclaim it and develop meaningful relationships. He was wealthy in the physiological and security areas, but starving relationally.

In another instance, an older, independently wealthy man paid a street-wise young woman regularly just for her company. Sex was a small if not absent aspect of the relationship. Simply being cared for and related to was sufficient for him.

After belongingness comes self-esteem. Self-esteem involves a sense of personal dignity and self-respect. I find it interesting that self-esteem follows rather than precedes belongingness in this model. In many cases, meaningful relationships cannot take place without a positive self-image. However, Maslow felt that one path to a healthy self-image is good relationships. If he is correct, then Loneliness In and Loneliness Out can prevent one from ever getting to the self-esteem level. In any case, because self-esteem necessitates knowing who you are and what your values are, Intrapsychic Loneliness is public enemy number one here.

The final level is self-actualization. This is a heaven-on-earth state involving self-fulfillment, the sense that one's full personal, occupational, and relational potential has been reached. According to Maslow, few ever attain this level, especially because it requires having successfully negotiated each of the previous four levels.

Although it has considerable merit, it is important to stress that Maslow's Hierarchy is only a theory. As such, a few comments may be helpful.

First, the model dooms the vast majority of people to less than full mental health. Indeed, if one has to climb up all five rungs of the hierarchy to be healthy, few will ever have a satisfying life. I don't buy that. I am sure you have known Christians whose dreams for earthly success have been shattered by illness or poverty, but who, nonetheless, experience a joy, peace, and energy unmatched by those we are taught to regard as successful by the world's standards.

Moreover, Maslow's Hierarchy does not address spiritual well-being. Those who dine on caviar and champagne, but are on a spiritual starvation diet, can hardly be considered self-actualized, no matter how good they feel about themselves or how satisfying their relationships are. Whether they realize it or not, they suffer from Spiritual Loneliness.

Nevertheless, Maslow's model can be helpful. It does highlight important human needs and can be used to see how loneliness can shortcircuit their satisfaction.

WHAT TO DO

The first step in overcoming loneliness is to realize that you have lots of company. You are not alone in feeling lonely. As I mentioned earlier, it is probably the most widespread psychological malady of our time. From singles bars to nursing homes, people are lonely. Ask anyone. You should live so long as to meet someone who does not experience loneliness.

Once you come to grips with how common loneliness is, you are ready to take step two: accepting it. That's right, choose it. Embrace it. Face it, you are—at least sometimes —lonely. You will not die from accepting it. In fact, the less you try to escape it, reject it, or deny it, the greater the likelihood that you will overcome it.

Loneliness may never become your friend, any more than getting up in the morning or balancing your checkbook— but it exists. It goes with being alive. It is here—present. Once it is accepted and embraced (not as a welcome feeling, but as a reality you are no longer afraid of), you have turned the critical corner.

Next, look at the types of loneliness described earlier, zeroing in on the ones that give you the most difficulty. We will discuss each type in detail later; but giving yourself an initial examination—a diagnosis—may reduce anxiety and confusion.

Doing a study of loneliness in Scripture is also valuable. There are two ways to do this. One is to find the various passages in the Bible that bear on the subject. You may not find a large number which address it directly; but with a little thought as you read and move through a concordance, you will find a number of very helpful sections.

A second way is to look at biblical models of loneliness with whom you can identify. Christ, Paul, David, Mary, and Ruth, as well as others, experienced extreme loneliness. Study these and other biblical examples, determining which type(s) of loneliness they confronted and how they handled it. This second method may help you find ways to overcome loneliness. But, more importantly, as you see how ancient and inevitable this condition is, it will give you people to identify with, and help you feel closer to God—realizing how aware he is of the pain of loneliness.

Once you have accepted loneliness as a reality—realized

it's a part of being alive, determined which type(s) you feel plagued by in particular, and looked into Scripture for additional help and understanding—you are ready to look more closely at how loneliness develops and to discover some of its effects.

CHAPTER 1

[1] Ruth Armstrong, "Christian Values and Self Psychology," *Encounter,* Spring 1982, p. 201.

[2] Abraham H. Maslow, "A Theory of Human Motivation," in Robert V. Guthrie, ed., *Psychology in the World Today* (Reading, Mass.: Addison-Wesley, 1971), pp. 101-119.

2
HOW LONELINESS
DEVELOPS

The little boy drifted away from home toward some railroad tracks. As a train ripped by, it blew out steam so hot that the youngster was scalded. The boy grew to become a poet and professor, but even in his adult years he had an extreme fear of leaving home and venturing out of his neighborhood.[1]

Early life experiences are formative. Often they are stamped into our psyche with the permanence of a footprint in wet cement. The effects of these experiences are not necessarily irreversible. But to overcome them, you need to be aware of them and their origins, and then make a conscious decision to meet them head-on.

Much loneliness is developmental. It begins in childhood and grows and develops much like the child's body does. In fact, many adult fears are simply "mature" forms of childhood insecurities. Indeed, the child *is* often the father of the man.

The renowned psychologist, Erik Erikson, noted how vital early experience is. In his theory of the life cycle, Erikson defined eight major stages of development.[2] At each stage there is a crisis—a psychological showdown—which must be resolved successfully for one to move on healthily to the next stage.

In infancy, Erikson's first and most important stage, the crisis is between trust and mistrust. If the infant is wanted, attended to, nurtured, loved, and conscientiously cared for in the very first year of life, he develops a sense of trust toward his environment. He feels that being alive is a positive experience and deals with it with a sense of security, peace, and healthy anticipation. The care he has received helps him trust others, give and receive love, and enter warm relationships.

If, however, the child is ignored, not wanted, cared for inconsistently, and neglected, a sense of mistrust and insecurity sets in. The outlook becomes one of fear, suspicion, and of course, loneliness. A child need not be abused to develop this lonely, alienated, mistrustful feeling—just not cared for lovingly and consistently.

If mistrust is the result of the first stage, the die is cast for lonely development. Dan is an example of this. For the first year of Dan's life, he bounced around through a series of foster-home and orphanage placements. He was a textbook case of poor early parenting, and developed a strong sense of what Erikson called mistrust.

At about sixteen months, Dan was adopted by a loving Christian couple. They placed him at the center of their lives, regarding him as a gift of God. Although when Dan came into their home he could not yet talk, with their nurturing care he developed into an extravert. However, the mistrust at the root of Dan's psyche did not disappear.

Despite his outgoing exterior, Dan was very insecure. As a child, he covered it over with bravado and aggressiveness. Though it camouflaged his lonely interior, his extravertedness worked against him. He became unpopular and caught up in frequent conflicts with his peers.

In high school, he secretly thirsted for popularity, but experienced little. Although he did have several close friends, Dan was generally unable to relax and be himself

26

with others, fearing a lack of acceptance. Instead he was loud, overbearing, and often critical. The outcome was loneliness.

College was not much different. Though talented and handsome, Dan had difficulty accepting himself, and hence, others. He used his looks, wit, and charm to effect a variety of whirlwind romances, but they all fizzled eventually. Dan relied heavily on his charisma to project a convincing but phony air of confidence, compensating for an inner loneliness and anxiety.

Dan's Christian life was one of struggle. Inability to feel close to himself meant inability to develop closeness with others. Since Dan experienced troubled relationships with the humans he could see, it is no surprise that he felt alienated from the God he could not see. Christianity was an erratic, anxious, guilt-ridden experience.

Thinking a Christian marriage would place him on the right path, Dan married in his early twenties. The marriage shattered, leaving him feeling guilty and confused. He had tried, but failed—miserably. God's grace was increasingly difficult to internalize.

In his thirties, Dan went into therapy. He began to see and grow out of his emotional immaturity. He began to realize how he had spent his life vacillating between a false confidence and illusory independence on one hand, and a holding-others-responsible-for-how-he-felt dependency on the other. Dan faced the fact that he had not come through the trust versus mistrust stage successfully, and he began working on dealing with the consequences of that. He began changing his inner vocabulary from one of "You make me feel..." (making others responsible for his emotional state) to one of "I feel..." (taking responsibility for his own life and well-being).

Dan still has troubles with intimacy and all-out trust, but he has turned the corner and is moving steadily toward a psychological life of trust, security, and openness.

There are a lot of Dans out there. They are black, hispanic, and white; upper, middle, and lower class. What they have in common, psychologically, are negative formative experiences.

Lytt Gardner shows how powerful the effects of early loneliness are, reporting research which indicates that children who are deprived emotionally suffer serious physical and emotional injury, even the stunting of physical growth. Dr. Rene Spitz found that infants who had lost their mothers suddenly suffered from "marasmus," a physical wasting away. Some who had lost parents suddenly refused to eat and died. Spitz, along with Katherine Wolf, studied ninety-one infants in foundling homes. These children, well cared for physically, did not receive adequate emotional nurture. Thirty-four of the ninety-one died, despite receiving good food and conscientious medical attention.[3]

Erikson's second stage, early childhood, pits autonomy against shame and doubt. In a child's second and third year of life there are rapid increases in muscular strength. If his parents give the child freedom to explore his newfound strength, grabbing and letting go of objects in his environment, he develops a feeling of autonomy—confidence and healthy self-assurance. If, however, the parents are overprotective and controlling, a feeling of doubt or shame emerges. The child becomes introverted and uncertain. And this going inside himself brings on feelings of loneliness.

Dina exemplifies this. As she was born out of wedlock, the other children in her neighborhood were not allowed to play with her. She grew up an isolated, lonely, and fearful girl. She felt negatively about herself and her abilities. It was not until at twenty-two, when she proved to herself that she was an able person (by being the first member of her family to graduate from college), that Dina developed the confidence to move without fear into the world.

Shame and doubt lead to emotional isolation. Instead of reaching out, you retreat into yourself. Shyness and loneliness, cutting yourself off from healthy relationships with others, are the likely consequences.

From age four to five, during the play stage, the child faces the initiative versus guilt crisis. No longer just imitating others, he is at the age of curiosity, moving around to explore his environment, imagining things, and fantasizing. The conscience begins to develop at this stage. It is important that his parents allow the child to develop initiative, feeling good about his new sense of discovery and curiosity.

If his parents play on his developing conscience by overburdening the child with "no-no's," "shame on you," and other messages of guilt and disapproval, he is in jeopardy of developing a negative self-image and a sense of guilt whenever he is disposed to venture out and explore.

It is right here that so many Christians get hurt. Conscientious parents, eager to teach their child moral truths—a clear sense of "right and wrong"—often go over the edge and instead communicate messages of disapproval toward their developing child. Controlling, restraining, forbidding, reproving parents naively do much damage to a child at this stage. Once that initiative is blunted and replaced by a vague but pervasive sense of guilt, loneliness is the sure result. A child who feels bad about himself, no less than an adult, is going to find it very difficult to love God and to respond with loving openness to parents and peers.

Treating a child as a miniature adult, spiritually, is both illogical and dangerous. I recall one Christian youth worker who, whenever he was upset at the behavior of some of the elementary grade students, would ask such questions as, "Is that the proper Christian attitude?" Not only was this method ineffective and guilt-imputing, but the children came to dislike him intensely.

During the school years, the battle is between industry and inferiority. The elementary school child, interested and fascinated by new learning experiences, wants to know the how and why of things. Whether learning to read, doing an art project, or building a treehouse in the backyard, the child is being introduced to the world of work and involvement. Encouraging, and in particular, recognizing and praising a child's efforts are vital here if he is going to develop a healthy sense of industriousness. Work and effort then become rewarding ways to invest his time.

If his efforts are criticized, regarded as messy and clumsy, or simply unrecognized, a feeling of inferiority sets in. One trip to your local grade school can make this crisis obvious to any observer. As you walk into the building, almost immediately you are confronted by a bulletin board giving recognition to students whose academic and personal behavior are considered superior. In my daughter's school there are citings for those on the Honor Roll, Eager Achievers (how about this one? an eager achiever is one who missed the Honor Roll by one mark), Superstar Readers, All-Star Readers, and Star Readers, as well as Good Citizenship award-winners. And that's just in the hall.

When I visited her Home Room I felt overwhelmed by the explosion of colors and decorations. Many of these recognize the accomplishments of the children who have performed well in the classroom.

In this type of environment there is no substitute for recognition. One child, who had carefully placed all her homework out for her parents to peruse on Parents-Teachers night, put her head down on her desk and cried openly the next morning because neither parent had taken the time to come.

With all the adulation heaped upon achievers, you don't have to be Sherlock Holmes to figure out how underachieving children, who are consequently unrecognized, are going to feel about themselves. A sense of inadequacy and inferiority seems almost inevitable.

Elementary school children are unlikely to admit to feeling inferior. Rather, they become rebellious or withdrawn, antisocial or shy—all certain pathways to feelings of loneliness and estrangement.

I know one small grade school child who covers his sense of inferiority by mischievously teasing and fighting with his peers. Feeling inferior to some of the popular nonwhite students in his class, he will make remarks such as, "I'm smarter than you because I'm white," and hurl epithets like "nigger" at them. More than inexcusable, these behaviors are pathetic evidences of how unhappy and alone the youngster feels.

There are psychological risks for the good student as well, for often he begins to tie his feelings of self-worth to achievement. Beth, an only child who lived with her mother, was livid over a B- I gave her on one of her assignments in my psychology class. She told me she tolerated nothing less than an A. She explained that she studied six hours daily—by the clock. Nothing less than perfection was acceptable to her or her mother.

I told Beth that, although she might get an A in my course (she did), she was cruising down a very self-destructive road. She was linking her mental well-being to grades —grades which were not directly under her control. What would happen, I asked, if an instructor—to teach her a lesson in life—were to give her a B? Since it is easier to get an amendment added to the United States Constitution than to force an instructor to change a college grade, she would be in deep psychological trouble. Beth had no answer.

I suspect Beth's mother unintentionally set up this vicious system. Wanting to encourage her daughter to be successful, she erected an outrageous standard. Its effect was to make her love and approval of Beth blatantly conditional. For Beth, the message was clear: she was a worthy person if she achieved, and a failure as a human being if she did not. So Beth became a slave to her teachers' red marking pencils and the tyranny of the clock.

In any case, what makes this stage markedly different

from the preceding three is that the child is now exposed to a much wider social world. He is no longer rooted exclusively in the home, but is now in school, clubs, church, community activities, etc., such that a larger number of people will have impact on him.

Identity versus identity diffusion is the adolescent's dilemma. With all the physiological, psychological, and social upheavals of puberty it is little wonder that most adolescents have trouble pulling together the loose strands of their identity into a coherent pattern. Yet that is precisely the challenge here.

If anything, resolving the adolescent identity crisis is more difficult than ever. In a technological age—with the multiplicity of life options discussed earlier, the breakdown of traditional values, and access to and involvement with more and different kinds of people—groping your way through to a stable sense of who you are is often a frightening challenge.

Edgar Jackson claims that "teenagers are in a state of normal neurosis."[4] Everything is changing, from their glands to the expectations of their parents and others. Moreover, popularity is longed for, such that "in-groups" are powerful social forces in adolescence. Being left out is exceptionally painful. I remember that I was riddled with emotional agony as a teenager whenever I felt excluded by my peers. The misery can be intense and depression may develop—a depression which increases loneliness.

Nevertheless, resolving this crisis will be more or less difficult, depending on how well you came through the earlier stages. Adolescent and adult problems often hark back to childhood loneliness. James Lynch refers to mountains of studies connecting a lack of parental involvement or early parental loss to later emotional insecurity. Early parental loss has been related to adult depression, dependency, psychoses, and suicide. Among adolescents, Dr. Roslyn Seligman found that 36.4 percent of the troubled adolescents with whom she worked had experienced some form of early parental loss. A study of 12,000 ninth graders in Minnesota indicated a relationship between parental loss and delinquency and dropout rates.[5]

If the identity issue is worked through successfully, a stable sense of self develops, giving the person a feeling of inner security, and readying him for independence and satisfying adult relationships. If the identity is diffused—blurred—the responses can range from an inability ever to take responsibility for his own life to assuming a rebellious, negative identity in order to feel some sense of significance.

Identity diffusion is a formula for loneliness of the most severe sort. It involves Intrapsychic Loneliness, Loneliness Out, and often Spiritual Loneliness. Many adolescents, left without parental direction, wander aimlessly in search of themselves or react aggressively to their confusion. Yet the other extreme is damaging too.

Monica was reared in a highly traditional, authoritarian home. Her parents controlled her through verbal hounding, household duties, and curfews. They even sent her to a nearby college—largely, I suspect, to insure that by living at home, the parental regime would not be toppled. They made certain she was a lonely child by selecting with excessive care the young people, particularly boys, with whom she could associate.

In any case, graduation from college brought Monica much more than a diploma. It sent her into a confrontation with the outside world for the first time. To enter adulthood, Monica needed to determine who she was, what her values were, and how to limit her parents' role in her life. She knew she would have to "make the break" from her clutching parents. Doing so, however, was sufficiently painful that she spoke with me about it only (and then, with reluctance) if I brought it up.

Adolescence is, indeed, a period during which parents feel they age markedly. For they have to allow the adolescent freedom for self-discovery and yet offer guidance to correct excesses. Erikson says that the teenager "needs freedom to choose, but not so much freedom that he cannot, in fact, make a choice."[6] For parents, this becomes one long series of judgment calls.

This is a critical stage. It is where everything from finding someone to marry to entering the work world begins. It is the bridge to adulthood and all the responsibilities adulthood implies.

If the adolescent does begin adulthood with an intact identity, he is ready to enter intimate relationships. These relationships, the principal one being marriage, are characterized by an emotional sharing which does not bring with it a fear of losing one's identity. Intimacy is set off against what Erikson calls isolation—loneliness. Dan, mentioned earlier, ran into all sorts of snags at this stage. While able to attract others, particularly women, he could not establish truly intimate relationships with them. His identity was not sufficiently stable to permit him to do so without being dissolved emotionally in them in a dependent, infantile fashion; or being easily threatened and so feeling driven and frantic in his efforts to maintain them. His relationships tended to be stormy, ending in bitterness.

In any case, inability to get through the earlier stages successfully programs a person for failure in the young adulthood stage—a failure which takes the form of loneliness, alienation, and isolation.

Erikson has two more stages: adulthood and senescence. In adulthood the confrontation is between generativity (concern with aiding and guiding the next generation) and self-absorption (selfishness and personal stagnation). In senescence, life comes to a close either with a feeling of integrity and wholeness, or despair and disgust.

In looking over Erikson's theory, we see the seeds of adult loneliness and alienation are sown early, in the developmental stages. In fact, Erikson claims that the negative of each stage is characterized by a form of loneliness—"infantile anxiety, fear of abandonment."[7]

EFFECTS OF LONELINESS

Although no one need tell us of the psychological pain loneliness can bring, its effects go much wider than that. A New York study of coronary patients found a significant number had lost their father to death between the ages of five and seventeen. Moreover, a study following up some 1,185 students from Johns Hopkins School of Medicine revealed that those who committed suicide, experienced behavior disorders, or developed malignancies had reported greater problems with interpersonal relationships and loneliness than the others.[8]

In fact, Dr. Lawrence LeShan found that loneliness and despair alter body chemistry destructively. He found that cancer patients, almost without exception, had a despairing, bleak outlook at the center of their lives, one which viewed life as hardly worth living.[9]

Edgar Jackson writes of a seventy-five-year-old woman who had skin cancer. In his conversation with her he found that her pet dog had died. The dog had been her constant companion, such that its death brought intense grief. She felt so relieved to be able to share openly her sense of loss with someone who listened empathetically, her symptoms cleared up and her treatments were postponed. Since leaving the hospital, she has entered a number of meaningful human relationships and has reported no recurrence of the cancer.[10]

James Lynch, in *The Broken Heart: The Medical Consequences of Loneliness,* presents much evidence supporting the notion that "brokenhearted" loneliness can bring on disease and death.[11] For those who do not deal with loss well, there is stress, poor appetite, erratic sleep, and a tendency to care for themselves poorly. The outcome of this is often physical deterioration, disease, and even death. Clinical research and mortality data have shown that human contact is a key factor in human health.[12]

Hospital research reveals that patients who have been moved out of intensive care units to other wards have more relapses than one would predict medically. This may be due to a feeling of abandonment over the sudden removal of consistent attention received during a period of great crisis.

Moreover, recovery rates in coronary care and trauma wards are higher for patients with friends and relatives who visit and show consistent concern. The simple holding of a patient's hand by a relative has been found to lower the heartbeat. In fact, any action that penetrates the loneliness of a fearful person has positive effects.[13]

It is assumed that reducing loneliness is beneficial because it reduces the stress associated with it. One study done in a metabolic ward, which focused on levels of serum cholesterol, showed that warm, caring relationships significantly lowered cholesterol levels, while stressful involvements heightened them. In short, medical studies have determined that simple human contact is significant. The heart responds positively to even the most common types of human concern.[14]

However, at the bottom line, loneliness is of critical importance. It is believed that feelings of loneliness and depression can have lethal effects. In fact, some surgeons will not perform serious operations on patients in depressed states because such patients often feel death is a better solution to their problems than improved physical health.[15]

Simply stated: People can get sick from feeling lonely; and if the feeling is severe enough, they can die from it.

WHAT TO DO

Take a serious, no-nonsense look at each stage of your life. Examine your life, going back to the very beginning. Look for loneliness as you would for a lost wallet. Whenever you think you may have uncovered a period or a specific experience of loneliness, try to focus on it, re-feeling the feelings. This will often be difficult. Your mind does not like to experience painful things any more than your body enjoys injury. Almost reflexively, you may find your mind darting away from the memory. This tendency of the mind to fight off and push away painful reminders is called repression; according to Freud, it is the most common of all the defense mechanisms.

Sheila is a walking example of this unwillingness to confront a painful past. Deserted by her parents in childhood, Sheila grew up in the streets. By the time she was a teenager, she was living all alone in Chicago. She moved in with some dope pushers who lived luxuriously off the narcotics they sold. Getting high regularly was the norm for Sheila and her friends.

For Sheila, the drug high was more than a drug trip; it was a trip away from the loneliness she felt. With her weight ballooning to over two hundred pounds, Sheila found herself getting rejected as consistently in adolescence as she had in childhood.

When I met Sheila, she was brimming with evidence of wanting to be loved and valued; but she covered it with an exterior of vulgar independence. She called and visited me regularly, but each time I asked her about her childhood she refused to talk. "I have no past," or "I do not exist," was the reply.

Poking a little deeper, she would deny all feeling. "Feelings make you vulnerable," she would say unemotionally, "and whenever you let yourself become vulnerable you get ripped off." She simply would not, under any conditions, face herself, her psyche, or her past head-on. It was too painful.

The price Sheila is paying for this is continued loneliness and depression. She will never overcome her psychological adversaries until she is willing to call their bluff by focusing on them. You cannot afford to be a psychological fugitive if you want to be free of loneliness. So, put the spotlight on your psyche and its experience with loneliness. Force yourself to get into it. Feel it. Explore it. Examine it.

To help you do this, I have included some suggestions for what you might look for at each of the first six stages. These are by no means exhaustive, but are presented to stimulate further exploration on your own.

Infancy. Find out what you can about the conditions surrounding your birth. For example, was your mother sick? Was she overburdened with a number of other things, making care for you sporadic? Was your father present in the family? If so, what condition was your parents' marriage in? Were you born closely to a brother or sister? Relatives and friends of the family can tell you these things. It is helpful to know all you can, for that first stage, passing as it does without our conscious awareness, is the most important.

Early Childhood. As you grew up, were your parents encouraging or were they overcontrolling? Did your father spend time with you, or was he too busy? Did you have brothers or sisters or friends to play with during those second and third years of life? Did you have an adequate play area? Were there plenty of toys?

Play Age. During the years of conscience development, did you develop a heavy sense of guilt? Did your parents emphasize the negative? Did your church put grace in small letters and sin in all capitals? If it did, you were probably breathing in guilt fumes by the time you went to Sunday school. More importantly, how did you feel about yourself? Did you see yourself as bad and evil—or valuable and worthwhile?

School Age. In school, were you recognized and rewarded; or were your efforts ignored? Were you involved and eager, or reluctant and lacking in confidence? And, if you were a good student, did you feel your value as a person in the eyes of your parents would plummet if you stopped achieving? If so, there was a lack of unconditional love and you were left with the lonely and neurotic task of earning your personal worth.

Adolescence. Did you have close friends in adolescence? Did you feel popular and accepted? What about teenage crushes? Did you experience adolescent heartbreaks? If so, did you suffer through them alone, or perhaps never really resolve them healthily? In short, do you remember adolescence as a lonely time, or as one of great fun?

Adulthood. Was intimacy—soul-opening—difficult in your early adult years? Were relationships hard to form, or keep? Do you live with the gnawing frustration of feeling there is so much more to you than you are able to share with others—or even are aware of yourself?

Once you have really "gotten into" the pockets of loneliness, study them to see if they set a pattern of future loneliness. If so, review your life frequently over the next few weeks or months, sifting through the effects of your loneliness. Do it thoroughly, because once you get a fix on loneliness, you will have taken a giant stride toward overcoming it. You will no longer be running from it. You will have met it face-to-face—stared it down—and survived. Instead of feeling insecure, weak, and scared, you will have, with mature strength, accepted it and proved yourself able to look at a highly emotional issue rationally and constructively.

However, even though you have delved into the origins of your loneliness courageously, don't expect the loneliness suddenly to grab a plane and fly away. It has been a long-term resident and so, although it may go underground for awhile, it will not want to be evicted. So continue to watch closely for every sign of it. Little insecurities, bouts with feelings of abandonment and isolation, and "blue days," are cues that it is resurfacing. You may very well detect patterns and "triggers" that stimulate feelings of loneliness.

The more you do this observing, the more you will be shifting away from reacting in a sheerly irrational, emotional fashion, toward confronting loneliness rationally. A great deal of loneliness will not stand up to rational scrutiny. You will realize that some of your loneliness is a form of illogical and unrealistic self-pity. In any case, even when you have logical cause to feel a bit lonely, you will not per- mit yourself to run from it—to let it control you—and become impulsive. Instead, you will be using your mental energy to decide logically what you want to do with it.

Some of your loneliness may not yield to your prayers, thoughts, and rational efforts. You may need to see a skilled therapist or pastor to help you handle loneliness and its effects. But you still will have moved off square one.

The more you do this self-examining, the better you will come to know yourself, and, as a result, feel comfortable with yourself. That in itself will reduce loneliness. How- ever, you will also be able to see through your loneliness and its mysterious hold on you will be undercut. In addi- tion, you will be more conscious of what activities work for you to overcome those sieges of alienation and isolation which intensify it.

You will become less anxious even in your loneliness. This, by itself, can move you forward dramatically, because it enables you to talk to others about loneliness without feeling self-conscious and embarrassed. This can lay an ex- cellent foundation for quality relationships as well as enable you to gain additional victories by helping others with their loneliness.

A key ingredient is prayer. Open your loneliness, and your need for help in tracing it, to God. If feelings of spiri- tual guilt block the path, tell him about that too, opening your soul as you self-examine. You will not only be bring- ing the power of God's perfect vision into your search, but, by being transparently honest with God, you will also be moving closer to him. There are many excellent books on prayer which can help in turning you loose; however, right in Scripture (Psalms, for example) there are many examples of soul-baring prayer with which you can identify and be guided in your time with God.

CHAPTER 2

[1]Clifford T. Morgan, *A Brief Introduction to Psychology* (New York: McGraw-Hill, 1977), p. 86.
[2]Erik H. Erikson, "Youth and the Life Cycle," in Don E. Hamachek, *Human Dynamics in Psychology and Education* (Boston: Allyn and Bacon, 1968), pp. 305-316; David Elkind, "Erik Erikson's Eight Ages of Man," in David Popenoe, *Sociology* (Englewood Cliffs, N.J.: Prentice Hall, 1974), pp. 124-128.
[3]Edgar N. Jackson, *Understanding Loneliness* (Philadelphia: Fortress Press, 1981), p. 49.
[4]*Ibid.*, p. 3.
[5]*Ibid.*, pp. 50, 51.
[6]Hamachek, p. 312.
[7]*Ibid.*, p. 308.
[8]Jackson, p. 51.
[9]*Ibid.*, p. 52.
[10]*Ibid.*, pp. 53, 54.
[11]*Ibid.*, p. 54.
[12]*Ibid.*, p. 56.
[13]*Ibid.*, pp. 56, 57.
[14]*Ibid.*, p. 57.
[15]*Ibid.*, p. 59.

3

LONELINESS
IN

Humans are the only organisms that experience loneliness. The reason is that we have what is called self-consciousness—an awareness of our own selves. You never hear of chipmunks with inferiority complexes or squirrels who suffer from a painful divorce. Their brains are not highly developed enough to experience self-consciousness; therefore, they cannot feel lonely either. So, despite all the blessings of being human—having a brain which can perform computer-like wonders and a capacity for sophisticated and enriching communication with others—we do have to live with the other side of the coin: the pain which comes from having a void in our social and psychological lives.

LONELINESS IN

The loneliness void is understandable when you are alone, but it is particularly painful when you feel as if you have the key ingredient necessary to be free of loneliness—a present relationship—and yet are still lonely. Jim, a forty-three-year-old businessman, was in a painful marriage for fifteen years. There was almost no sexual involvement in the relationship. "My wife told me flat out that I was a lousy lover," said Jim. "We became not-so-friendly roommates for the sake of the kids," he added. Jim's wife had several affairs which eventually ended the marriage. Jim now lives alone and is not involved in any intense relationship.

"Yet, I am less lonely today, living alone without a relationship," says Jim, "than I was all during our desolate marriage."

Loneliness In occurs when you are in a relationship, expecting that your social and emotional needs will be met within it, yet facing the cruel reality that you are still lonely —desperately lonely, despite the presence of another in your life. One of the great illusions of our age is that simply having a relationship—any relationship, whether romantic or friendly—will combat loneliness. In reality, unfulfilling relationships often intensify loneliness.

Ellen, forty-eight, living with an emotionally handicapped husband, experiences an acute form of Loneliness In. "Doctor, we have no adult communication, haven't had for thirty years," she said, breaking down on the phone. "I am more his mother than anything else. I can't leave him. I'd feel too guilty to do that. He needs me. He can't survive without me at all! But I am just desperate to talk to someone —an adult who will listen and understand me. I don't expect you to solve my problems; I am not looking for miracles. Just someone to talk to," she sobbed.

Let's go on with Ellen's story. "I am so frustrated and live in such emotional pain!" she cried. "All my feelings are pent up and I am not able to express them. I have found an outlet in writing poetry and doing other creative writing, but it is not enough. I am becoming very angry, bitter, and resentful."

HOSTILE FEELINGS

Angry, bitter, and resentful. When you find yourself experiencing Loneliness In it is very difficult not to harbor these poisonous feelings. These are common responses to Loneliness In because you feel ripped off—cheated. After all, you entered a relationship, have given yourself to it, and were willing to endure the tragedies as well as the triumphs. One thing you never imagined you would have to endure, however, was loneliness. It seems so unfair.

If your partner is unaware of your loneliness and seems to be doing quite well himself, the loneliness is accentuated and the hostile feelings become intensified. The most common way people deal with these feelings is by avoiding them, pushing them back in their minds, even denying (at least to their partner and often to themselves) their existence. Giving the feelings room for expression is frightening; you feel you may lose control.

Pushing them under never works. They corrode your personality and give rise to increasing venom. Moreover, a damaged relationship cannot be restored amid these feelings. If your partner does make a move toward you, it is difficult to notice, much less accept, when there is a cauldron of hostility inside.

The first step, if you are experiencing Loneliness In, is to examine your feelings. This takes courage and willpower because often our minds try to skirt away from looking at things which are not positive. But it is imperative. Look right down the barrel at your feelings, not just at the Loneliness In (you know that exists), but at how you feel about that loneliness. If you spot hateful feelings, don't deny, repress, or rationalize them away. If you do that you have wasted your time self-examining. Also, don't feel ashamed, frightened, or upset; just accept yourself. Acknowledge to yourself that you are angry, bitter, and feel ripped off. After all, lots of people experience these feelings when there is Loneliness In.

Once you have confessed them to yourself, open them up to God. Tell him how hurt and angry you are and how you want to be delivered. Don't "dress up" the language or feeling. Let out the venom you realize is destructive and need to be delivered from.

Now comes the difficult step. If your partner is at all open to listen, simply tell him about the process you have been through: you have experienced great Loneliness In, and this has given rise to resentment and anger. Not wanting to feel these feelings, you have admitted them to yourself and before God. Now you are admitting them to your partner. What you would like (but are not demanding) is to talk with him about the loneliness you've been experiencing and what you, together, may be able to do about it.

Although it is vitally important to tell your friend or loved one about the loneliness, few people do. Instead, they harbor the hurt inside, hoping for something to change the situation. Whenever I'm on radio call-in shows, I receive calls, one after another, from people filled with the pain of loneliness and lack of relational fulfillment. I always ask the same question: "Have you shared this with someone?" "No," is the answer; they have never considered being so vulnerable. Unless it is shared, nothing good can happen.

TYPES OF RELATIONSHIPS

To deal with Loneliness In, we need to understand that there are different types of relationships. In essence, we can distinguish three kinds of relationships: impersonal, personal, and antipersonal.[1]

Most of our relationships are impersonal. They are marked by practicality rather than intimacy, fueled by what each member can do for the other. They have a businesslike quality, based on mutual self-interest.

The impersonal relationship may very well contain a good degree of friendliness and good feeling, for over time its members come to like and appreciate the services of one another. However, these alliances are founded on mutual self-interest, rather than emotional closeness.

The personal relationship is the one we all strive for. It is the closest and most intimate one. As desirable as it is, however, the personal relationship is not always easy to develop. There are, in the society itself, contemporary forces which work against effecting intimate, close relationships.

SOCIAL FORCES

One of them is materialism.[2] The emphasis on accumulating wealth and material possessions runs the risk of making things more important than people. We become consumed with achieving and using, leaving people neglected. Moreover, we are so busy moving and doing, we have little ability to relax and be with others.

Feelings are put on the back burner so that we are unfettered in doing our work. In fact, professional people are encouraged to put away their feelings so they can perform their tasks effectively. However, the deeper our feelings are buried, the harder they are to become aware of and comfortable with; and of course, the less we are able to communicate at an intimate level.

With materialism comes competition.[3] Instead of relating to, understanding, and caring about others, we must confront and defeat them. Competition necessitates that we not be vulnerable. So, emotions are repressed in the heat of the chase. We become so conditioned to competing that we try to avoid emotional involvement at every turn. After all, to be transparent with someone with whom we may have to compete would make competing with that person much more difficult.

Competition can go on within the closest of relationships. In marriage, spouses compete for time, status, and attention. Friends do subtle and open battle over points of view, schedules of activities, and prestige.

Linked to materialism and competition is individualism.[4] We live in a society that values individual rather than group accomplishments. We want our uniqueness affirmed, recognized, and celebrated. Individualism stands over against relational closeness. It's the invulnerable, self-made, and self-sufficient person, not the loving couple, who is on the cover of magazines, in the headlines, and on TV.

PERSONAL RELATIONSHIPS

A personal relationship can take the form of a romance or a close friendship; but whatever its form, its principle characteristic is intimate, mutual sharing in a socially secure environment. This mutual exchange of intimacy is at the root of the personal relationship. Without such private disclosures, a relationship either never was personal or is becoming impersonal, with Loneliness In developing.

MUTUAL SHARING

Sharing is a two-way process. A personal relationship must be reciprocal to survive. Although an introvert and an extravert may very easily develop a close friendship or love, the amount of verbal sharing may not be equal; there must be some intimate disclosures coming from both people for their relationship to be personal.

Listening is not enough. If, then, you find yourself sharing intensely private matters with someone who listens intensely, even comments on them, it is even more important that that person share some things in return. If he doesn't, you may be dealing with a rather exploitative individual, one who likes playing amateur psychiatrist, hearing others' concerns without ever opening himself up in response.

If you are trying to develop a personal relationship, it is helpful to realize that people are often afraid to make the first move. After all, most of the personal information we share involves things we are unsure or even ashamed of, the stuff which shows our humanity and weakness. Some relationships never get out of the gate because neither person is willing to take the risk of initial vulnerability. Take the lead by sharing something moderately intimate. Throw something out there to see how receptive the other person is. If, after several such attempts you get no caring response, you have a clue that a personal relationship is not in the offing and you can move on.

However, if you are burdened with Loneliness In as part of an unfulfilling relationship, you need to take the risk of opening up to have any chance of it developing into a personal one. You may have to take the first step—or, in a marriage, many steps—by revealing who you are before someone will share in return.

Moreover, through the sharing a great deal of identification develops, and this ability to place yourself mentally in the position of the other further strengthens the sharing aspect. With our individual identity—our uniqueness—most distinct and clear in this type of relationship, it is little wonder that (in an age in which we are more often known by our serial, computer, or Social Security number than our name) we would seek intensely personal relationships.

If you are confused about a relationship, one way to tell whether it is personal or not is to determine the level of approachability. A personal relationship involves unlimited approachability, allowing you to call your friend or loved one any time simply to talk, without having to justify the reason for your contact. A personal relationship should also allow for touching and nonsexual physical contact. Physical closeness is a sign that you are comfortable and happy in one another's presence.

RULES

In any personal relationship, the environment must be secure. Each person must guard zealously the confidence of the other. If at any point you feel your partner is not discreet, you will stop trusting him and your relationship will deteriorate.

However, security goes deeper than keeping confidences.

It also includes the assurance that nothing vulnerable that is shared will ever be used as ammunition in a conflict. The following argument, the likes of which you may have heard often, is a perfect example of how this aspect of security can be violated.

"I am so tired of your jealousy I could scream. It seems that you want to possess me," hollers Bill.

"You're crazy!" Mary shouts back. "It's just that you pay so much attention to your friends—most of whom are women, I might add—that I wonder if you care about me at all."

"Oh, yeah? If you weren't always so uptight about me, I might spend some time with you. But you are strangling me with your possessiveness. You told me just last week about how insecure you are, how afraid you are of losing me. Boy, were you ever right! What you need is a psychiatrist, not a husband!" shouts Bill angrily.

"I'll never share my feelings with you again, Bill," says Mary quietly.

Once Bill let go with the "how insecure you are" stuff, something died in Mary. What he did is turn something very vulnerable, very precious, into a weapon. Mary's trust in him vanished like chalk being erased from a blackboard. The relationship went on the critical list and Loneliness In was on the horizon.

Antipersonal moments—times of conflict and discord—are almost inevitable in any personal relationship. Friends and lovers do have arguments, so rather than try to avoid them, it is important that you and your partner observe certain rules to keep your relationship from irreparable damage.

One is to agree never to use any of the truly vulnerable, intimate matters against each other in an argument. Such use must be considered unfair and any violation must stop as soon as it is noticed.

Another is to focus your negative comments on your partner's behavior rather than his character.

"I become really upset whenever you question me about where I was," sounds a lot different from, "Why are you so paranoid that you have to keep checking up on me?" The first deals only with the behavior—the questioning; the second labels the person mentally ill.

This rule is very difficult to follow because often we become so angry, so emotionally involved, that we want to strike out at our partner, hitting him right in the center of his self-esteem, dishing up a portion of the same pain we are feeling. Even when the arguments begin on behavioral turf, they can degenerate into mutual character assassination.

"I wish you would be less messy around this house," says Dorothy.

"Look, I try," answered George, "but I have a lot of work to do and the space you give me doesn't remind me of the Mojave Desert!"

"Don't tell me about space and work," Dorothy shoots back. "This kitchen, in which I spend half my life, feels like a phone booth!"

"There you go, complaining again. Complain, complain, complain. You're just like your mother. You're even starting to look like her," says an angry George, hurt because he feels put down over Dorothy's remark about the home he provided for her.

"Man, you can't take anything, can you?" says Dorothy. "One little complaint and you get paranoid, thinking you're being attacked."

"Well, if you would just grow up yourself and stop griping all the time, I would be a lot happier," responds George.

What happened here? Dorothy and George have long ago stopped discussing the behavior of neatness and are now taking shots at one another's self-esteem. Dorothy started out well, zeroing in on a troubling behavior, but down the road became frustrated and slipped into the paranoid label. George was no better—he tried to level her with the emotional maturity rap.

By telling Dorothy that if only she'd stop complaining, he would be happier, George violated a third rule: Never hold others responsible for your own feelings. This is important because telling others that they *make* you unhappy has an attacking quality and will stimulate defensiveness. Their behavior may be wrong, but how you respond emotionally is within you, and is *your* choice. Ten different people will respond in ten different ways to the same behavior.

But what if your partner clobbers you personally? Simply ask him to stop. "I know you're upset, but I wish you would talk about what I did and not attack me personally," is a good response. If you want to slip in an "I don't do that," it's OK, if it's not done self-righteously. If you consistently follow these three rules, it should pay off eventually and eliminate a good deal of Loneliness In. Your partner may violate rule number three—holding you responsible for his feelings. But that can be dealt with in calmer moments.

ACCEPTANCE

Fundamental to the personal relationship is a relaxed atmosphere of mutual acceptance. If this acceptance is undercut, the relationship is impaired.

Dean and Charlotte lack consistent closeness in their marriage. One of the problems is that Dean was reared in a very strict religious home, while Char was not. So, whenever Char opens her feelings to Dean, he unintentionally but automatically runs what he hears through his religious-belief filter. As long as what Char says squares with Dean's value system, everything is OK. However, when something questionable hits his filter, Dean's warmth dissipates and he becomes distant. For Char, this is lonely stuff. Instead of hearing and nurturing her inner self, Dean is judging and evaluating her.

The price of judgment is Loneliness In. Christ, knowing

this, shows us a better way. He loves unconditionally—in spite of rather than because of who we are. Whenever people opened their real selves to him, whether it was the "fallen" woman at the well, or someone hampered with a physical disability, he responded with love, acceptance, and gentility. He always touched the person emotionally and spiritually, if not physically; and his strongest admonition was a caring, "Go and sin no more."

When people share their deepest feelings, they are not asking for an evaluation: just love, acceptance, and relief from the loneliness they feel. The words you say in response (and often even what they say in revealing themselves) are less important than the unspoken requests: Love me; care about me; I am lonely.

COMMUNICATION

Sharing implies communication, and in the personal relationship the communication must far exceed chit-chat: "Aren't these appetizers divine?" John Powell emphasizes that truly intimate relationships must include two communication levels in particular.[5] One is called the "gut level." Here the stuff of communication is feelings. This level shatters the intellectual barrier, moving from the head into the heart and soul. Exchanging ideas, judgments, and thoughts is not enough for a strong personal relationship to develop. Head level communication is the *milk* of human interaction, when what is needed is *meat*. Although it can be risky to share our feelings, they are what give us our uniqueness.

Even beyond the feeling level is what Powell calls "peak communication." This occurs when, out of gut-level communication, people suddenly experience a sense of total unity and oneness. These moments, as few and temporary as they are, are among the most rewarding in life. They do not come, however, without a price; that of opening up and breaking through the intellectual walls.

MEN

Men often have much more difficulty sharing their feelings than women. While women tend to be "processors"—able to accept, express, and feel their way through emotional pain—men are often "fix-its," focused on solving problems which are being expressed in emotional terms. They are often threatened simply by exposure to emotional discomfort.

Carla drew a very insightful distinction between her mother's and father's responses to emotional pain. "If I go over to see my parents and I'm depressed, my mother will listen to me and then just let me feel my way through the pain of the day as she goes about her business," she explained. "My father will listen, but with great anxiety that he has difficulty hiding. It seems as if he just has to give me advice, hoping it will solve the problem and shut me up. Although he means well, he does it to help himself more than me. One time, after I had been feeling blue for several days, he said, 'You gotta stop that crying. You're upsetting your mother!' " Carla ended with a laugh.

Earl has been a lifelong pillar in his community. Whenever there are tragedies, people come to him and talk. Invariably, after people pour out their feelings to a patiently listening Earl, he very calmly and acceptingly gives advice. An elder in his church, he often gives excellent counsel. Though he is very skilled and helpful to many, Earl's relationships are one long series of Loneliness In. He is known deeply by no one. His family relationships have been impaired by this conviction that what people want is advice. For years his son Mike longed to get close to Earl, to be known and loved by him. Mike's efforts took the form of baring his soul, confiding the frustrations of his inner life to Earl, in hopes that he would be loved just as he was. Unfortunately, what Mike received was not unconditional acceptance and affirmation in his pain, but rather advice.

Earl is like many men, a classic fix-it. He simply cannot

coexist with painful feelings. He needs to repair them and make them go away. So, though he is revered as a model person and family man in his community, Earl remains a lonely man.

Men are threatened by feelings largely because they have been taught as children not to cry, not to admit weakness, not to be scared, not to be nervous—not to feel. Feelings are a mysterious enemy they must crush to avoid being overwhelmed. Feelings are foreign to many men, so that when women close to them seek emotional contact and intimacy, they feel an indefinable shock of anxiety. Authentic relating is threatening. It demands a behavior of which they do not feel capable. It removes them from their perch of invulnerability and control, tossing them into the threatening sea of unresolved feelings. Withdrawal becomes the only answer.

I knew one minister who was inordinately skilled in every aspect of his pastoral charge, except dealing one-to-one with his parishioners' feelings. He tended to refer most of his people to the church's counseling center. Though he loved and respected his wife greatly, he used workaholism to avoid moments of close, vulnerable communication. Fortunately, he realized his problem and is dealing with it effectively.

MANIPULATION

"It's just useless. Whenever I open my feelings up to my husband, he doesn't respond. I don't think he even cares," says a frustrated Linda.

Talk to her husband and this is what you will get: "Linda just dumps all her stuff on me, and if I don't agree with her, tell her I love her, or give her the exact response she is looking for, she becomes angry."

When sharing demands a certain response, it becomes manipulation. In fact, it is not sharing, it is entrapment.

Real personal confiding is characterized by just that, opening up at the feeling level without in any way restricting the other person's freedom to respond. If I share with you, desperately looking for a particular kind of supportive response, you will feel trapped and nervous, realizing that if you do not give me the emotional answer I am demanding, there will be conflict. Out of that anxiety you will avoid personal moments with me, thus fading the relationship to a more impersonal tone and introducing Loneliness In. Sharing our feelings must be a gift, not a demand. If you want a certain response, simply express the desire—don't demand it.

SELF-ESTEEM AND SELF-ACCEPTANCE

The main reason we fall into this demand tendency is that we hook our self-esteem to the response we receive. When our self-esteem is shaky, we are without a proper psychological foundation from which to accept others and relate lovingly.

In fact, the most common cause of the antipersonal relationship is threatened self-esteem. Therefore, whenever you look to others as the source of good feelings about yourself, you are in a high-risk zone. Depending on others to give you a sense of self-worth and significance not only makes you a victim and puts pressure on your partner to deliver the desired response, but when you don't get the feedback you want there is disappointment, pain, and often anger. A feeling of being put down emerges. At this point, defenses are marshaled and you want to go for the jugular.

Antipersonal experiences can be so painful, particularly for those who have less than sturdy egos, that they are often avoided at all costs. Larry, so anguished over frequent marital battles, unwittingly transformed his personal relationship into an impersonal one. "We had so many fights, so much conflict," Larry explained, "that the only thing I could do was avoid contact." Avoiding contact brought on

Loneliness In, followed by an affair which ended the marriage.

Reducing your demand level can eliminate much Loneliness In. This is especially important in marriages and other man-woman relationships. One reason we often get along better with our friends than those we are linked with romantically is because we expect less of our friends. We do not hook our self-esteem to their every response. The pressure is off.

A good way to take the demand out of personal relationships is to widen your relational circle. Friendships are invaluable here. Finding people with whom you have mutual interests and hobbies, taking courses which enable you to meet people, and getting involved in others in church and in your community are healthy ways to steer clear of the pit of obsession that so quickly develops whenever we feel Loneliness In over an unfulfilling relationship. Even if the circle-widening does not solve the problem in a key relationship, it will reduce the tendency toward "hooking"—extracting your feelings of happiness and well-being from your partner's responses.

Moreover, the simple inability to share at the feeling level is often related to a lack of self-esteem and self-acceptance, something we will discuss at length in chapter 5. Self-acceptance is not the same as self-approval. There are many sins and flaws in our characters which hardly merit approval. However, once we fall into the ditch of self-rejection and self-hate we never get close enough to who we are to work on our weaknesses.

We disguise our self-hate in a variety of ways. One common tendency is to project self-hatred outward, to see our own loathsome characteristics in others. Another, when the guilt of hating others is very intense, involves what Freudians call "reaction-formation." We show extreme forms of care and love for someone in order to assuage the guilt we feel over our hostility. In still other instances, we repeatedly compare ourselves negatively to others. This may yield a double payoff: (1) a feeling of absolution by condemning ourselves and (2) the reception of assuring messages from others that we are worthy and valued.

COMMON LONELINESS IN PRODUCERS

Clearly then, we can bring on Loneliness In through our self-defeating psychological tendencies. In fact, there are a number of very common destructive behavior patterns, many of which emanate from classic defense mechanisms against which we need to be on guard.[6]

Displacement. Displacement is scapegoating. Our lives are filled with frustration coming from sources against which we are powerless. As the barrel of hostility fills, we have to find some place to empty it. Where better than on those closest to us? Unfortunately, we rarely tell those we live with that our pain is coming from another place, so they feel hurt and defensive.

People who have difficult or unfulfilling jobs, problems with parents or in-laws, or money problems are especially vulnerable to displacement. Pain, anger, and frustration have a cumulative quality, and unless we can pour them out—to God, to others, or both—they have powder-keg potential. We may explode with an outburst, or simply let our hostility leak out through nagging and complaining.

Victor, brought up in a very strict home, had gone through a divorce. When he entered a relationship with Alice, he felt occasional guilt over the divorce, such that he didn't feel really free to be involved with her. The guilt would become so intense that if Alice would say the slightest negative thing about his former wife, Victor would explode. It was classic overkill, and it so frightened Alice that she wondered if she should remain in the relationship. Victor compounded the problem by not telling her about its origin for fear that Alice might think him prudish, or even end the relationship because he was not really committed to her. Victor never did tell her, and the relationship did not last.

More common is displacement, in which we are afraid to admit the real source of our anxiety and so focus on something minor as a cover. For example, a woman may feel sexually neglected, but because she feels too self-conscious to admit it, she complains about her husband's tendency not to go to bed at the same time she does. In both types of displacement we may or may not be aware of it, but the result is the same: It drives away those close to us, leaving us with Loneliness In.

Projection. Projection, mentioned earlier, is so common that it merits additional comment. The first recorded case of this "seeing in others what actually exists in ourselves" is found in Genesis 3:12, where Adam lays all the responsibility for his eating the forbidden fruit on "the woman you gave me," Eve.

Don had great trouble with sexual faithfulness. Any time he went to a movie in which there was a scene involving sex out of marriage, or saw a popular magazine with articles about sex in it, he got turned on. His wife, though not approving of sexual promiscuity, had no real difficulty with faithfulness, and so could keep such things as movie and magazine exposure in perspective. Because Don was ashamed to admit his problem, however, he projected it on his wife, accusing her of sanctioning immorality every time she suggested a movie or brought home a popular magazine. His projection produced alienation, hurt their sex life, and brought him much Loneliness In. Things did not get better until he mustered the courage to be honest and work out his problem with her.

Any time we hold others responsible for our feelings we are projecting. All those "you make me feels" are projections. This is not to deny that certain feelings are rather common responses to other people's actions. Nevertheless, if we do not take responsibility for controlling our own thoughts, and therefore the feelings that arise from them, we are not being mature and responsible.

Rationalizing. The rationalizer is bound to have trouble with personal relationships. He is simply never wrong. There is always a justifiable reason for his actions. The danger of rationalization is that if it is done often enough with others, it becomes an internal mental pattern; and pretty soon we not only fool others, but ourselves as well. The rationalizer is often someone with a great deal of repressed guilt. The guilt is so heavy that the admission of wrongdoing or improper motives is psychologically paralyzing. Hence, he will, at all costs, try to work his way out of a feeling of sin. The brighter a person is, the better a candidate for rationalizing.

The best way to break the rationalizing pattern is to admit to someone you trust something that you attempted to rationalize. Once you have admitted it, you have taken the ultimate and irreversible step in dealing with it. You have removed any possibility of deceit and made yourself accountable to someone else at the same time. This is particularly effective if you struggle with a specific problem. Opening it to someone neutral—a pastor, therapist, or accepting friend—is the ideal first option because it makes you accountable to someone you trust who will help you overcome rather than deceive yourself and others with the problem.

If you begin to turn the rationalizing pattern around by confiding something of import to someone you trust, you will also discover that others are not as judgmental as you. After all, it is your judgmentalism that has driven you to rationalize. The relief you will get from the grace extended by others will help open up more and more areas to honesty rather than rationalization.

If you live with a rationalizer, the most important thing you can do is to be accepting—nonjudgmental. Curiously, this is very difficult because the temptation is to pierce through the other's rationalization and get at the truth.

However, if you are nonjudgmental and then model openness by revealing areas of wrong and weakness in your own life, your chances of gaining new honesty and closeness increase.

Always Right. A close relative of projection and rationalization is what Powell calls "Always Right." This person cannot lose an argument under any conditions. He will debate to exhaustion without admitting defeat. The reason is that he must win in order to survive psychologically. The Always Right is usually suffering from rather deep-seated doubts and uncertainties, whether conscious or not, and so he needs to be right in order to persuade himself and remove the anxiety he feels over his lack of faith. Indeed, he does protest too much.

Robert, a middle-aged man, was gentle and accepting on the exterior; however, whenever a religious issue came up he always had a position—the right one. No matter how obscure the passage or minor the theological point, he clutched to his interpretation. Notwithstanding his low-key and seemingly polite style, he was either talking or waiting to talk. He never listened, except to find holes in his opponent's argument. At times, there was an almost hysterical and desperate quality to his argumentation. He couldn't survive being wrong.

A clue to Robert's problem is that he was raised in a rather stern, highly doctrinal and legalistic home, where one's standing with God depended on correct doctrine and proper behavior. Robert paid a real price for his correctitude. Despite his genuinely caring spirit, his relationships, even in his own family, were never close because he never allowed himself to be human enough to be at the level of his loved ones.

Never Angry. The Always Right may also be "Never Angry." He has nothing but caring concern for others. This Never Angry facade hides the hostile feelings inside—feelings we all have, but which are particularly frightening to him. Those around Never Angry do not really feel close to him because they can't identify with such a "saint." They admire and respect him, but do not feel intimate toward him. Though Robert exemplified a Never Angry, this tendency is more common in women because of our society's "sugar and spice" expectations that women are not to have hostile or vengeful feelings.

If you have trouble with being "Always Right" or "Never Angry," it is likely that you haven't internalized the love and grace of God, in addition to having cut yourself off from the love and acceptance of others. Red penciling the biblical material on grace and forgiveness, coupled with reading books that deal with God's love and acceptance, is a good road out.

If you live with someone afflicted with these problems, don't argue with him. All you will get is tired. Instead, without giving in to the person's preachments, begin to model openness and humility. State your beliefs in a speculative, "I don't know all the answers, but..." way and let him see it is possible to be wrong but loved.

Pouting. The pouter really generates Loneliness In. Here the inability (due to embarrassment or hostility) to discuss his grievance leads the pouter to sigh and mope sullenly, bringing as much unhappiness as possible to those he is with. Though it is a passive, quiet strategy, pouting is very powerful and is felt keenly by those in the pouter's vicinity. Its strength lies in its tendency to frustrate others without allowing them to deal openly with the problem. It is quiet, siege warfare.

The pouter will self-righteously point out, "I didn't say anything!" when others refer to his hostile behavior. But he realizes the alienation he produces by punishing those around him. It is enormously self-defeating, because neither the pouter nor those in his presence are happy and there is a continual movement toward resentment and anger rather than resolution.

Pouting is self-pity linked with a desire to punish others. It is also unfair. Learn to express your feelings using the guidelines we mentioned in discussing the antipersonal relationships. Take responsibility for your own emotions, even admitting that they may seem silly to others but are real to you; and focus on the behaviors about which you are upset. You don't have to win any argument. Feelings are not grist for who's right and who's wrong. They are simply how you feel about what is happening.

Taking the monkey off the back of others by owning your feelings is more likely to get the response you want than digging in your heels and radiating silent hate. You might begin by saying, "I am tempted to pout about this, but I don't want to. I feel. . . ."

Every one of these Loneliness In producers has the same quality. Each produces a power struggle between people who should be sharing lovingly. This generates competition rather than cooperation, winners and losers rather than friends and lovers. But this is common, due to the selfish streak in human nature. For that reason it is important (1) to be on guard against these patterns in your own life at all times, and (2) if you see them in others, don't give in to self-righteousness. You would not recognize them in others if you didn't have the capacity for them yourself. Think of loving ways that will help your partner out of the pain he is obviously experiencing.

It's OK to confront those you love, but this confrontation must be on an, "It seems to me . . ." or "I wonder if . . ." level, rather than a, "You always have to be right," or, "Why don't you stop dumping your guilt on me?" plane. And when you do confront in a speculative this-is-how-it-seems-to-me-but-I-could-be-wrong way, don't be surprised if they deny it. You have lost nothing. What you have done is planted the seeds of openness, patiently hoping for a harvest.

BECOMING IMPERSONAL

Larry (mentioned earlier) and Amy were married for four years. Despite many stormy moments, their relationship endured. However, after repeated arguments, Larry felt intimidated and resentful and gradually stopped opening up to Amy. Amy would occasionally share personal things with Larry; but with her busy work schedule those times decreased as well. With pleasantries every morning, "I love you" exchanges each night, and regular attendance at church and social events, neither was consciously aware that their relationship was dying. But both were experiencing Loneliness In.

Then Larry met Rita, a very attractive young married woman who showed interest in him. Rita's marriage was characterized by the same lifelessness Larry's was suffering from. Despite attempts on both people's parts to avoid getting involved, an intense affair began. Their closeness was euphoric and their sex dynamic. They were convinced they were meant for each other. Larry's marriage ended in a bitter divorce from a shattered Amy, while Rita, realizing that this was more puppy than real love, bailed out of the affair just in time to save what was left of her desolate marriage. Larry had traded Loneliness In for Loneliness Out, while Rita returned to her vacant Loneliness In marriage.

Larry and Amy's marriage illustrates how easily and imperceptibly a personal relationship can become an impersonal one. The intimate sharing dries up, defenses quietly build, and the communication degenerates into conventional chit-chat and "head stuff." The partners spend less time together and experience decreased emotional involvement. Arguments may become even fewer as neither person is easily emotionally aroused. There may be a superficial overlay of friendliness used by both members to deny reality. Eventually, however, one of the partners wakes up, senses the deadness full force, and wonders, "What happened to us?"

Relationships like this can drag on for months and years, as long as their members live under the illusion that somehow the relationship will magically recover its freshness. Without awareness of the present state of the relationship, along with a commitment to restore its lost vibrance, change will not come.

SECRETS

According to Paul Tournier, what produces so much Loneliness In and impersonality are secrets.[7] Fear, doubt, regret, and psychological pain are kept concealed, hidden under a veneer of confidence and purpose. Living with a neatly camouflaged inner cauldron of unfulfillment and anxiety sprouts Loneliness In of the most intense sort.

Opening this up to our partner seems more frightening than usual, because we are in effect telling him that we have been trying to deceive him with a persona of cool all these years. Often our fears are unfounded, as the case of Eloise indicates.

Eloise, thirty-nine, spent her entire life being efficient, caring, and helpful, but never vulnerable to others. It gave her a sense of being needed and respected. She developed the reputation of being a psychological and social "Wonder Woman." All the while, her marriage was falling apart, despite her frantic efforts to maintain it. Feeling exhausted and unable to keep up appearances, Eloise gasped to me, "I can't go on this way. I am worn out and don't know where to turn."

"Why don't you tell one or two of your friends," I suggested. "They could be of great support at this time. Pouring out your heart to them, especially after all the help you have given, could be very therapeutic for you. Certainly, as strong-willed as you are, you will not become unhealthily dependent on them by doing that."

"Dr. Claerbaut, I just couldn't do that. I can't. You see, they all view me as 'together Eloise.' They lean on me. In fact, they would be so freaked out if they knew that the smiling, caring Eloise had a problem, I could never face them again," she said anxiously.

Eloise experienced Loneliness In in every relationship.

She had many friends who loved and admired her, but she was a stranger to every one of them.

Fortunately, Eloise did have genuine friends. Eventually, when she took the risk of confessing who she really was to some of them, she experienced the care and redemptive love she had been living without for so many years. The honesty was liberating, removing much of the exhaustion that living a lie had produced.

The amazing thing about opening up—to our partner in a hurting relationship or to other friends—is that people are generally much more accepting of our weaknesses than we are. In fact, because everyone has frustrations, conflicts, and inner hurts, hearing of someone else's pain often dispels some of our own loneliness. Few will put down such an open person, for to do so is to put themselves down. Instead, the response is often acceptance and love.

LOVE

Love, however, is one of the most misunderstood and overused words in our vocabulary. Joan was in an intense relationship with a man. She spent every available moment with him, neglecting everything else from friends to hobbies. She built her entire life around him because that's what he wanted. The reason he gave for controlling her every move was that she was so important to him and he loved her so much. After six years, he ran off with another woman.

Although love may include voluntary commitments, it does not mean possession and demand.

Love is not dependency, or the manipulation that goes with it, either.

Darrell was a very insecure young man who covered it with a strong, cool exterior. Unwittingly, his relationships would follow a very predictable pattern. They would begin with his being very open to a woman's feelings, even sharing some of his own to accelerate the disclosure process. As the woman became more trusting, Darrell would begin manipulating her into becoming dependent on him. Once that dependency was in place, he felt safe.

However, because he had been pursuing the relationship for the wrong reason, Darrell would begin experiencing a great deal of Loneliness In. Feeling the woman wasn't quite right for him, he would begin to manipulate and dominate her, trying to remake her into what he wanted. Inevitably, the relationship would become intensely painful for the now confused young woman and increasingly unsatisfying for Darrell as well. The relationship would end with the woman feeling very hurt and bitter at Darrell's lack of acceptance, while he remained puzzled as to why he couldn't develop enduring, intimate relationships.

Darrell's problem was that he was not comfortable enough with himself to function without a relationship. He used relationships to deal with his own dependency. As such, he did not relate to others in an honest, mature, and open way. The result was Loneliness In, then manipulation, and ultimately Loneliness Out.

Love is letting your partner know you as fully as possible and being open to knowing him equally well. More importantly, it means helping your partner become everything he wants and is able to be.

In the spirit of 1 Corinthians 13, Tournier invests love with other characteristics as well.[8] Love, he says, is disinterested. It is not, as we discussed a bit ago, loaded with concerns about response. It is, instead, to be marked by openness and honesty. Love is also spontaneous. It flows from the heart rather than being dredged out of obligations.

Neal went with Karen for four years. After much vacillating and Loneliness In, he realized he loved her more as a friend than as a prospective marriage partner. Fearing the truth would hurt her, and feeling guilty about his romantic passion, Neal did not tell Karen the truth but rather tried to program his feelings in a romantic direction. It didn't work. Instead, Neal felt burdened by guilt and obligation. Finally, he told Karen the truth, which brought both of them a sense of liberation.

Love wants the best for another. Being on time, speaking in words your partner feels comfortable with and can understand, avoiding his pet peeves when you are able to, and behaving as though his well-being is genuinely important to you are examples of this characteristic. Such actions communicate love more powerfully than words.

Roger dated Doreen, a graduate student, for several months. The relationship became rather intense, appearing as if it might have lasting potential. One evening Doreen told Roger she was facing a difficult period in school and would need more time to study. She stated that she would not be seeing him at all during that time. Roger felt rejected and angry. Although they did see each other after the hiatus, their relationship was never the same and ended shortly after.

Roger and Doreen's experience illustrates that love involves time. Time is among the most precious commodities we have, particularly in our high-voltage society. Time indicates priority. Although consideration for another's schedule is important and a part of wanting the best for the person, a relationship cannot grow without the investment of time.

In as demanding an age as we live in, one of the best ways to have relational time is to schedule it just as you would anything else. Whether it is scheduling family days with your spouse or outings with a friend, working out a schedule to be together—one which nothing short of a national emergency would be allowed to alter—is helpful.

THE BOTTOM LINE

The bottom line in overcoming the pain of Loneliness In is to realize that personal fulfillment comes from within. No one else can make you happy or fulfilled, or make your life worth living. You were created by God as an individual who has the capacity to relate to others. Others should *add* to your life; they do not *make* it. To allow someone else to become your "whole life" is a form of idolatry. It is unfair to the other, as it makes him responsible for your emotional well-being, as if he were some sort of psychological life support system. And, of course, it turns you into a victim. You become a mere responder to him and totally at the mercy of his treatment of you.

You are responsible for your own happiness, fulfillment, and well-being. Others can contribute, but you are responsible for taking care of yourself. If you are in a negative relationship, you have to decide what you are going to do about it. If it is with a friend or married partner, it is your responsibility to confront the situation caringly. If it is a marriage to which you are committed for the rest of your life, and it seems hopeless as far as meeting your intimacy needs, you need to look at what appropriate alternatives you have to meeting those needs. The ideal situation may be out of reach, but you can improve your life if you take action to do so.

People who feel depressed and hopeless—both of which accompany much Loneliness In—tend to get better when they realize that there is something they can do about their lives. If you are experiencing a great deal of Loneliness In, feeling your life is doomed because your relationship is not working, you are probably depending on that relationship to fulfill you. You need to take responsibility for your own life by placing that relationship in its proper realistic position: as an important but not all-encompassing aspect of your life.

You have to make the changes. Laura called in to a radio program. She said, "I've been married seven years and I am bored with my husband and life. When I am with him, I imagine he is another man, a more exciting man," she said. "How can I change him so he'll be the kind of man I dream about?"

"Have you talked to him about your feelings?" I asked.

"No."

Not only had Laura not been honest with her husband, she also ignored a basic rule of human behavior: People will not change unless they want to. Trying to change others, even for the better, is not love. It is manipulation. Wars have been fought since antiquity for civic freedom. Certainly individuals want the freedom to be who they are personally, as well. Trying to change others unilaterally is self-defeating and unloving.

The only thing that you can do is to tell them how *you* feel (not how they *make* you feel, but how *you* feel), and see what can be worked out. If they care about you, there is a good chance they will attempt to make some alterations in your direction. If they can't, they may at least be sensitive to how you feel—and that, in itself, is often enough to remove the discomfort. If they refuse, there is nothing you can do to change them. Nagging at them, humiliating them, and putting them down only tires you out, stimulates anger in them, and makes them less likely to change.

FINAL NOTE

So, if you are experiencing Loneliness In, remember you have lots of company. Christ faced it with his erratic, ignorant disciples 2,000 years ago; and the divorce courts are filled with it today. It's painful but common. Look at yourself critically. Look at your relationships carefully; determine, if you can, what is at the root. Then, laying aside those all-too-easy-to-believe illusions that matters will change by themselves, assess your options (you always have some, so look for them), take responsibility for yourself, and act.

CHAPTER 3

[1]Unpublished research by S. Kirson Weinberg in David Claerbaut, *Social Problems, 2,* (Scottsdale, Ariz.: Christian Academic Publications, Inc., 1977), pp. 52-54.

[2]Edgar N. Jackson, *Understanding Loneliness* (Philadelphia: Fortress Press, 1981), p. 139.

[3]Paul Tournier, *Escape from Loneliness,* trans. by John S. Gilmour (Philadelphia: Westminister Press, 1977), pp. 30-49.

[4]*Ibid.,* pp. 50-86.

[5]John Powell, S. J., *Why Am I Afraid to Tell You Who I Am?* (Niles, Ill.: Argus Communications, 1969), pp. 57-85.

[6]The following destructive behavior patterns are derived from *ibid,* pp. 103-158. Powell's book is an excellent source for dealing with relational problems.

[7]Tournier, pp. 45-46.

[8]The following characteristics are from Tournier, pp. 113-116.

LONELINESS
OUT

"Are you married?" I asked Irene, the perky fifty-year-old woman sitting next to me on the plane.

Without saying a word, she pointed to her left hand. Then she said, "Actually, I'm married now, but I don't live with my husband. I've given up on relationships. Now I just sit home, watch TV, and eat."

Later, when I remarked, "I can't imagine a bright, vibrant, and attractive person like you giving up entirely," she emptied out her pain in one sentence: "There's no one who loves me anymore."

Irene is suffering from Loneliness Out, the feeling that there is no one out there who really knows, cares, or understands her. It is among the most common yet painful human experiences. You feel abandoned, rejected, and isolated—all of which give rise to a sense of uselessness, a what's-the-point-of-going-on feeling.

THE BROKEN-HEART SYNDROME
There are many causes of Loneliness Out. One is the loss of a valued relationship through death or breakup. If you have suffered a relational loss it is difficult to dispel the Loneliness

Out until you have worked through the stages of that loss. Although a thorough discussion of the stages in the broken-heart syndrome is beyond the scope of this book, it may be helpful to outline some of the main stages involved in a breakup (though they are often identical to those in a loss through death), offering some suggestions which will speed resolution.[1]

The first stage is one of shock. There is an I–can't–believe-it quality to it. You feel numb, emotionally paralyzed. You hardly cry or experience any intense feeling. You are left cold. Yet the loss is gradually being registered, and although you feel coolly logical, you probably are not. For that reason, the number one thing to keep in mind when the numbness sets in is not to do anything impulsive. Don't suddenly call him, send her flowers, make wild concessions if only she will resume the relationship, or any other such thing. It is almost invariably self-defeating. It will not get you what you want. It only adds humiliation to the pain. If you have any friends at all, turn to them immediately in this stage, because they will be rational buffers for your actions. Going it entirely alone, as tempting as it is, is a formula for self-defeat.

The second stage is one of grief. There is agony, excru- ciating emotional pain—knowing that something that has been so central in your life is gone and you are without anything to replace it.

Don't try to stonewall the grief or be brave. Cry it out. Just as the stomach rejects poisoned food, you need to expel the pain emotionally. Grieve until you can't anymore.

If, however, this stage becomes prolonged by constant crying and feeling sorry for yourself, try this method. As corny as it may sound, set a crying time each day. Then go about your business throughout the day, knowing when- ever you feel blue, that at 8:00 P.M., you can grieve it all out until you are satisfied. Setting and adhering to a crying time is therapeutic because it is the first step in getting control of your feelings. Moreover, you will probably find that sometimes when your crying hour comes, you won't feel like grieving anymore, realizing that it is a waste. Then you know you're on the way to recovery.

In this stage, there are two other important things to do. One is psychological; the other is more concrete. The psychological task is to accept that the relationship is over. He is gone. Though he may return, you must assume he will not. That is extremely difficult, as hope does tend to spring eternal. But it is a must. As long as you hold out hope, the pain will remain. Whenever you lapse into dreaming of some reconciliation, check yourself with a quiet "no" and go back to what you were doing. End it.

A good way to speed the psychological process is to perform the concrete task of getting rid of the triggers. Remove all of the things that remind you of the lost loved one, whether gifts, records, souvenirs, pictures, whatever; get rid of them. Cleanse your environment of his memory. You needn't destroy or give the stuff away if you don't want to. Just put it out of your view. Also, do not talk about him. If a friend calls and says, "Guess what, I saw Wayne last night at the store," break in with: "Please, I'm trying to get over the pain of losing that relationship, so if you want to help, try not to mention him to me if you can."

The grief stage is the toughest, but if you work at it with an iron will, you will move through it more quickly.

Often there is an anger stage in the process, too. You feel put down, abused, taken advantage of. You are enraged. Don't punish yourself for feeling this way. Anger is not necessarily a sin. How you handle it is what is important. If you nurture it, it can be prolonged, hurting only you.

A woman called in on the radio and told me she was, after years, still incensed about her former husband. "I feel so ripped off financially," she said. "I'm left with nothing after all these years."

I suggested the same thing to her that I mentioned earlier in the grief stage. Schedule an anger hour. Move through your day, knowing whenever you feel angry that it is more stuff to use during your raging time. Then let loose on schedule. Scream, cry, insult, punch your pillow, and throw things, letting every fiber of anger roll out of your system. After doing this for a while, as with the grief period, you will no longer feel like doing it. You will realize not only that this will not bring him back, but that it is taking up precious time you could use doing something else. Moreover, now that you have regularly poured it all out in concentrated explosions, much of the angry energy is gone anyway.

This emission of anger is important. You cannot forgive someone else until you have worked through your anger and hurt. Sealing up the hostility and putting on a smiling face is self-deluding. Responsibly confess and expel your anger so you can, with integrity, forgive and ultimately forget.

The last stage is resolution. Here the pain and anger are under control, and you are ready to return to the land of the living. There is a freshness, a starting-over feeling about this stage which makes it a very pleasant experience.

The key to moving through the stages at a steady pace is self-discipline. Giving in to the temptation to park yourself on the couch and feel sorry for yourself, forgetting your crying hour and letting loose whenever you feel the pain, or wallowing in the memories of a lost relationship by living surrounded with triggers—all will retard the process enormously. Remember, every time you let down you hurt only yourself. If you want to recover, you have to fight.

LONELINESS OUT PERSONALITY STYLES

Often people experience Loneliness Out simply because they are unable to form close relationships. This requires self-examination. You may unintentionally be turning others off. Powell discusses several self-defeating personality types, which are helpful to review.[2] Look at yourself critically to see if you have any characteristics of one or more of these styles. If you do, don't be ashamed; you have lots of company. They wouldn't be written about if they weren't so common. However, understand that they repel others like lotion does mosquitoes.

One relational repellant is dependency. We talked about this earlier. The *dependent* looks to a relationship, usually a romantic one, to *make* his life meaningful. There is no more common, yet destructive tendency than this. We are surrounded with messages which reinforce dependency. Virtually every popular song dealing with feelings encourages us to be dependent: "You're Nobody Till Somebody Loves You"; "You Are My World"; "You Are My Destiny"; "You Are My Happiness"; "You Make Me Feel Like a Natural Woman"; "You Are the Sunshine of My Life." Though people can bring joy and happiness into our lives, they cannot *make* us happy, much less become the only source of our happiness.

First, as we indicated in the previous chapter, such an outlook makes you an emotional puppet, giving others God-like power over your psychological well-being. And like a puppet, if the string ever breaks, you collapse. Second, you will probably drive other people away with the smothering effect of your dependency.

Dependent relationships often begin very euphorically. The dependent person has his needs met and the person depended upon feels like a potentate, a tower of strength. However, over time the stronger person loses respect for the weaker, feeling the crushing weight of the weaker's dependency. He feels suffocated and begins wanting out. The weaker, sensing imminent loss, responds with even greater desperation and dependency, driving his partner away.

If you are dependent, as unhappy as it may seem, you may be better off without a relationship—because the probability is that any relationship will burn out, leaving you with a broken heart.

The best antidote to dependency is to build your self-esteem. Therapists, books, and even friends can help you do this. However, a good way to start is to determine how and where you began to develop this dependency. Whenever it began it was probably because you doubted the validity of your own ideas and feelings, looking to others to accept you.

Once you know where it started, you can begin to build your own internal self-confidence at the feeling level. Whenever you feel a certain way, but wonder how others would regard those feelings, say to yourself several times, "I have a right to my own feelings," or, "My feelings are as valid as anyone else's." Begin owning and claiming for yourself your thoughts, ideas, and feelings. Then, as you gain confidence, begin expressing them to others as they are.

Whenever you feel you are becoming vulnerable to someone else, ask yourself whether you are going to choose to be or not. If you decide to enter a relationship, make it a choice, not a desperate grab at feeling good about yourself. And if you choose it, realize that person is not *you*—only an important person in your life. He is not responsible to take care of you emotionally, just to treat you well and with respect. Also, realize that relationships do end and that you are choosing to face that if it happens. Dealing with people on an adult plane of mutual respect and sharing has to be the goal.

Closely related to the dependent is the *romantic*. The romantic brings on his own loneliness by not relating realistically to others. He lives in an emotional Disneyland, filled with the fantasies contained in popular songs and in gothic romances. No one can possibly fulfill those fantasies, and so the romantic's unrealistic expectations guarantee disappointment, rejection, and loneliness.

There is dependency in the romantic, because he depends on his partner to make him feel romantic. More importantly, there is a shortage of realism. Romance and romantic moments are important parts of love relationships, but only parts. There are also mundane aspects of making a living, paying the bills, and coping with daily annoyances. Like an impatient child, the romantic often cannot accept this side of relational life, and so becomes depressed.

Enduring love relationships commonly go through three phases.[3] The first is euphoria—the feeling of being in love, when the world is beautiful and energy is unending. Here the focus is totally positive. This is followed by disillusionment—the realization that your partner is a flawed person like yourself, and being involved with him means accepting those parts of him too. There is a growing awareness of the incompatibilities that exist. The focus shifts to all the negative elements. The final phase is realism, one in which the positive and negative dimensions are maturely balanced off —in a state of equilibrium. Here the partners come to know, respect, and appreciate one another as fellow humans who are making the best of their lives together.

The romantic rarely gets more than an inch into phase two. Either his partner becomes annoyed with him and pulls out of the tangle, leaving him devastated; or, realizing the flaws in the other, he ends it himself and sets sail, looking again for the relational equivalent of the Holy Grail.

The *clown,* with his jolly, life-of-the-party behavior is in hiding. He entertains in order to be accepted, but cannot deal honestly with the painful aspects of life. Although the clown gains superficial popularity, it works against him. Because people do not see the clown as a serious person, available for a personal relationship as a friend or romantic partner, but rather as a jolly soul who needs no one, the clowning *prevents* rather than facilitates people getting close to him.

Many clowns are unaware of why they do their routine. If you tend to be a clown, realize that the exit door is the one marked "Facing Reality—and Sharing It with Others."

The *competitor* wins all the battles, but loses the war. He wins every game, every argument, every award, but loses in relationships due to his two-dimensional character. He never allows himself to become open, vulnerable, and human enough to be related to as a peer. The competitor has two problems. One is that he feels a lack of self-worth, owing to a lack of approval in early life, and so goes about trying to win it; second, he confuses himself, as a person, with his accomplishments. He *becomes* his accomplishments —a thing rather than a person. If you're an achiever, look carefully at the reason why. If achievement is a healthy outgrowth of your productivity and energy, be thankful for the gifts God gave you; if it is to prove something to yourself and others, realize you can never achieve enough to feel you have proven yourself adequately. Moreover, you are distancing yourself from others by your frenzied quest for achievement.

Guy, a middle-aged performer, was a *crank*. Though having a great capacity for warmth and charm, he complained about everything. His golf game was never good enough; the President didn't know what he was doing; his wife got on his nerves; and the younger performers ought to go back to being bat boys. As a crank, Guy poisoned every meaningful friendship he had.

Cranks like Guy are very insecure. They're uncomfortable being themselves and relaxing, so their defense is to lash out at the injustices of the world. Not only does Guy not know *why* he is a crank—I doubt if he even knows that he *is* one. But if you recognize this trait in yourself, understand that it repels others. People are aware of enough misery in the world. They don't want to hear your contributions. Facing your insecurity and following the same steps suggested for improving self-esteem can be helpful.

Cranks are often *cynics* as well. With a sarcastic wit, they comment insightfully on how flawed everything is. Archie Bunker is a disgruntled cynic. He is also a textbook case of the cause of cynicism. His dreams have not been realized and he feels ripped off. He agrees with John F. Kennedy's observation that life is unfair. However, unlike JFK, who accepted it and adjusted to it, Archie munches the bread of self-pity and resentment. The cynic's loneliness arises from two sources: he hides his true feelings of disappointment and vulnerability under a witty exterior and others don't want to be around him because he is such a "downer."

Dean, whom we met in chapter 3, is a *dominator*. He has a compulsive need to run the lives of others. He would enter a friendship or romance very charmingly; but once in it, he began taking over the reins—not just of the relationship, but of the very life of his partner. For Dean and thousands like him, domination masks dependency. Dean needed rather than wanted a relationship. Once in one, he "secured" it through domination. Depending on the situation, his methods included trying to coax dependency out of his partner by showing her care in moments of vulnerability; undermining her self-concept and confidence through criticism; and leaving the impression that she never quite pleased him. Anything to bring her under his control. He could do everything but love her and be honest with her. Eventually the women in Dean's life would terminate the relationship, leaving him with a strong case of Loneliness Out.

The dominator hides his weakness with a show of strength. His front can be very convincing if he is practiced at it. The front is necessary because he has never felt safe and loved as a vulnerable person. It is difficult to muster much empathy for the dominator, but usually that is what he needs.

The way to break the domination syndrome is to realize that it is a pattern of weakness rather than strength; to acknowledge it to others (if possible, to the person who is your victim), and commit yourself to be as honest as possible in the future. This takes a great deal of courage because what the dominator fears most is rejection—loss of the person on whose love he wants to depend. But the payoff is well worth it. If he chooses honesty he will be respected for his openness and his possibilities for intimacy will be greatly increased.

The *hot dog* is a short-fused person who explodes with overkilling rage. His anger is out of proportion to the acts which trigger it. Almost without exception, hot dogs have an ocean of pent-up hostility which floods over when incidents ignite their tempers. Often they have been frustrated in their childhood but had no outlet to vent their anger and pain. So, in adulthood, they compensate with outbursts. Much of the rage comes from an accumulated generalized hostility, while some of the rest of it owes to stored anger against the target person. Their problem is that instead of acknowledging feelings of anger as they are experienced, and in proportion to the situation, they harbor anger and then pull the trigger at unexpected moments.

If you tend to be a hot dog, look at your past carefully, working through your rage at your parents (the most likely sources), or others who are at the root of it. (It can be valuable to get help from a therapist to do this.) Further, practice expressing your anger in the moment, and in a controlled way. Counting to ten before exploding; asking yourself whether the person at whom you are angry deliberately set you off; and breathing slowly and deeply when feeling anger, in order to get the physical excitation under control, are excellent ways to regulate your anger.

Saying, "I feel angry because..." rather than, "Why are you such an inconsiderate...?" will work wonders. It is a way of owning your own anger, reminding yourself that it is in you. And it lessens the likelihood of defensive behavior on the part of the other.

William is a *"messiah,"* who is loved by everyone. His door is always open to help anyone in need. When people land in the hospital, he visits them. When a neighbor is ill, he brings her flowers. When there is a crisis, he is ready with wise counsel. But William is a loner. He confides in no one, and seeks help from no one. No one is at his level of virtue and altruism.

What makes William a "messiah," and hence a generator of much Loneliness Out, is not his kind deeds. It is his motivation for these deeds. He must at all times overcome his feelings of inferiority by presenting himself morally above others. He will not allow them to help him, and so display his own vulnerability. Such an expression is very frightening because William is afraid that he will not be liked as he truly is. This fear grows out of a vast reservoir of repressed guilt he is terrified to face.

Getting out of the "messiah" trap is helped by desensitization. Pick someone—just one person—you trust, and tell him you have fallen into that role. Open yourself up to him to whatever extent—however small—you are able, and begin to receive the acceptance and love he gives you. Once you have done that, continue to practice openness with others (even strangers you may meet and may never see again, so you don't have to fear future self-consciousness), taking gradual steps until you can be open to the ones you love.

Joining a group of other people of the same personality type for the sole reason of sharing your inner selves in a safe, accepting environment can be very beneficial. If you live in or near a city, there is usually a variety of such groups available. Calling a therapist, consulting the newspapers, or talking with friends may lead you to such a group.

The *worrier* sets himself up for Loneliness Out. His constant talk about possible calamities drives people away like skunk odor for three reasons. First, people don't like to hear more bad news than they already are exposed to. Second, the worrier almost invariably focuses on *his* problems, making him a rather self-centered, selfish person; finally, after you listen to a worrier and offer him wise advice, you can be sure of only one thing: He will be back soon with a new list of worries.

Excessive worry translates as emotional immaturity. Worriers are self-centered people who are looking for others to take responsibility for their lives. They need to practice handling crises so they can, on one hand, experience some confidence-building success; and, paradoxically, on the other, face enough failure so they are no longer traumatized by it. What they do not need is someone to listen to them, reinforcing their self-defeating pattern of *reciting* problems without facing up to them.

SYMPTOMS

Two common symptoms of Loneliness Out are depression and boredom. Depression is dangerous because it usually means stagnancy—sitting around and doing nothing. Instead of confronting the world, you intensify your loneliness by sitting home, where, unless you receive a phone call or visit, you are most assuredly going to worsen the condition you want to avoid.

There are many explanations for depression. You may be turning hostility inward on yourself. You may feel hopeless about key issues in your life, or you may simply be feeling sorry for yourself. In any case, it is a common malady and one you must fight through activity. As Dr. Wayne Dyer puts it, "You can't bounce a ball against a ball and be depressed at the same time."[4] However, the feeling of immobilization in depression can be so strong, you feel welded to the chair, unable to pick up the ball. But you must choose to move or it will worsen.

We feel bored when the stimulation level in our life is too low. We are at a blah, lonely intersection with depression around the corner. Boredom is something you choose by telling yourself negative things and remaining inactive. Again, to recover, movement is vital. In the case of both boredom and its more severe counterpart, depression, there is a tendency to see life from a victimized, "poor me" perspective. As long as you feel life is *making* you bored or depressed and hence, lonely, you will remain so. When you decide not to feel that way, recovery has begun. A good way to move yourself out of the psychological paralysis is by making a daily schedule for yourself, one which forces the activity and involvement you need, but feel no inclination toward.

Richard, fifty, a once famous entertainer, was depressed for five years. Convinced it was due to a chemical imbalance, he underwent every medical procedure available to uncover the problem. After finding no organic cause, he landed in my office.

"Doctor, I'm so depressed. I can't read, write, listen to records, talk to a woman on the phone, or even take a shower," he moaned.

Looking for sympathy, he received none. "You can do all those things," I said, "you just *won't.*"

"I can't," Richard responded.

"Nonsense. You tell yourself you can't, so you won't," I answered.

"Well, I feel great discomfort when I do those things," Richard explained.

"Basically, you have two choices," I stated. "One, you can choose to face the anxiety and discomfort you experience, and force yourself to do the things you want to do but tell yourself you can't; or, two, you can choose to remain stagnant, depressed, and suicidal."

"Believe me, I get so depressed, I just can't do anything. And, what's worse, I am so terribly lonely," Richard protested mildly.

"You can take a shower," I announced, "You are not going to die from standing under a shower, are you?"

"Well, no, but I do feel uncomfortable," Richard replied.

"Fine, we'll start with the easiest task," I said. "You will face the discomfort and take a shower every day."

"OK," Richard mumbled, "I can do that."

He did. Soon he was listening to records again. The journey for Richard is one of shifting himself—step-by-step—out of "park" and into "drive" by forcing himself to do the things he wants to do but has told himself he can't. The more active Richard is, the less depressed he is.

On the other extreme from stagnancy is impulsiveness.

This is a common, but risky response to Loneliness Out. There is a frantic grabbing after something to remove the dead feeling that accompanies Loneliness Out. Although spontaneity is good, impulsiveness is self-defeating. It suggests a tendency to leap into an activity—any activity—without weighing its consequences. Disastrous relationships, calamitous business deals, and tragic accidents are the offspring of impulsiveness.

Another Loneliness Out "disease" is telephonitis. Calls are placed to make contact with the external human world. Unfortunately, when people are not home or are unable to talk, the lonely person experiences an instant shot of disappointment and perhaps resentment, coming from a, "Boy, no one is ever around when I need him" feeling.

Colleen, twenty-eight, felt lonely in her depression and anxiety about never finding the right job. Her only relief was to call her married sister. However, instead of her calls indicating movement on her part, they were thinly disguised dependent cries for help. After a deluge of such calls, Colleen's sister asked her not to call anymore. Colleen's case illustrates that although using the phone can be a sign of activity and can alleviate much loneliness, becoming a telephone junkie is self-defeating because others start expecting and even dreading your calls.

If you are lonely and want to reach for the phone, it is wise to keep your calls reasonably short, unless the other person is equally desirous of talking. Remember, when you are calling only to relieve your loneliness, you are not likely to be the most stimulating conversationalist. So don't drag out the call, hoping to drum up some conversation. If you are calling a good friend who invites you to unload your pain, fine, but if it is a casual acquaintance who is accustomed to less intense discussions, try to stay on a more interesting track.

Another Loneliness Out tendency is to load up on radio and television. Although these media can occasionally provide excellent companionship, a total diet of such electronic stimulation is unhealthy and can even intensify loneliness. After a while, you begin realizing that, except for call-in shows, the voices you hear and faces you see do not respond directly to you in any way. They don't even know you're out there. It's this awareness of the impersonal nature of these media that makes them less than a panacea for loneliness.

JOHARI WINDOW

One theory that is helpful in understanding how intimate relationships develop is called the Johari Window (see Figure 2a).[5] The Johari Window indicates that there are some things that are known to ourselves. For example, I know my own name, my goals, my past, my fears, my anxieties, my age, etc. However, there are also things unknown to me. I don't know many of the people who will read this book or their impressions of it; I don't know all of what even my best friends think of me.

Figure 2b shows that there are also things that are known to others. Others know my name, where I live, my interests, my past, even some of the intimate things they have observed or I have told them. But there are other things they do not know. They don't know fully what I think of them, the things embarrassing to me, or, of course, many of the things of which I am uncertain.

You will notice in Figure 2c, that the Johari Window has four slots. One includes the things that are known to me and known to others. That is the open part. There are also some things that are known to me, but unknown to others. That is what I conceal in the hidden slot. In addition, there are some things that others know about me, but I don't know. This is the material I am blind to. Lastly, there is the stuff about me, which although it exists, neither I nor anyone else has yet discovered. This rests in the locked section.

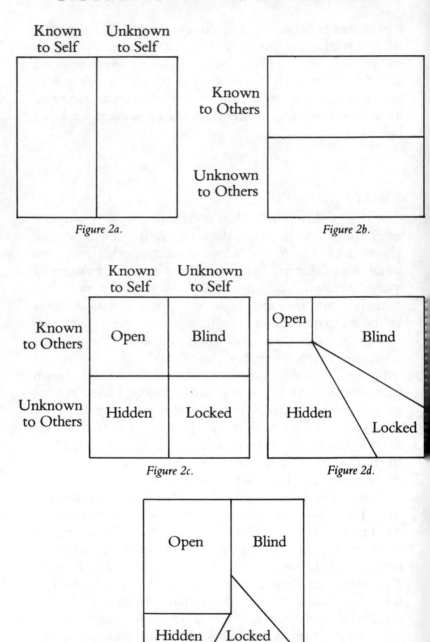

Figure 2a.

Figure 2b.

Figure 2c.

Figure 2d.

Figure 2e.

88

Figure 2d indicates that the typical person is not really a healthy person. The typical individual has very little open, much more hidden and blind, and a good deal locked. A Johari Window of the typical person shows us why so many people are lonely.

Ideally, we should have a great deal open, and correspondingly less hidden, blind, and locked, as shown in Figure 2e. This does not mean that we are open to everyone about everything; just that with key people in our life, there is a much larger open pane in our Johari Window.

To open your Johari Window, you have to begin moving material out of that hidden area. This involves self-revelation—telling others truly significant things about yourself. Every term, I ask my class this question: How many of you have really wanted to tell another person something significant about yourself, but just couldn't muster the courage to do it? Invariably, 90 percent of the hands go in the air.

"Why?" I ask.

"Because I am afraid of what they will think," says one.

"You could be rejected," another rejoins.

"I just don't want to make myself that vulnerable," is another's comment.

When you strip it all away, there are essentially two reasons why you are afraid to reveal who you are. One is that you don't like yourself. We don't enjoy talking about subjects we don't like. For example, if you don't like baseball, chances are you don't engage in many baseball conversations. Similarly, if you don't feel good about who you are, you probably would just as well avoid revealing your inner self.

The second reason is that you fear others will not like you if they find out what exists behind that public mask you wear. Here you may feel you have dug yourself into a hole. You have developed an attractive front, which suggests you are a much different person than you actually are. Let's face it—most of the heavy material people conceal is stuff they are not particularly proud of. If you depend on the good opinion of others for much of your self-esteem, you don't want to blow that good opinion, even if it is based on less than accurate data.

Actually, these two reasons are two sides of the same coin. In reality, reason number two—you are afraid others won't like you—is really just a restatement of the first reason—you don't like yourself.

Look at it this way. If you were truly stable in your self-concept, really felt consistently comfortable (not necessarily approving in every case, just comfortable) with who you are, then others' less than positive attitude toward you would not have such a jarring effect on your self-image.

Try this example. Think of your favorite food. Let's say it's pizza. Now, imagine that your best friend does not like pizza. Would you change your good opinion about pizza? Of course not. You would still stuff yourself with that Italian delight.

Yet, if your best friend were to dislike something significant about you, you would probably not feel as comfortable and accepting of yourself as before. That's the point. Often we are more certain of the worth of our favorite food than we are of our own selves.

The most important factor in self-revelation is self-acceptance. Translated, that means that you will not let anyone else's response affect how you regard your own worth. Once you break the self-acceptance barrier, you are home free—literally. You are home in that you can feel comfortable with anyone. You are free because you are liberated from the tyranny of others' lack of approval.

Self-acceptance does not imply that you love yourself in some self-contained, narcissistic, chest-thumping fashion. Just that you can live with yourself, accept yourself and who you are—faults and all. You are not punishing, rejecting, or nagging at yourself; you are accepting, taking care of, nurturing, and trying to improve yourself. Indeed, others' responses are valuable. They teach you new things about who you are and show you how to grow into the kind of person you want to be. They are never, however, a barometer of your worth nor a basis for being able to accept and be comfortable with yourself.

Self-revelation for those of us with fragile self-concepts is risky. It carries with it a fear of psychological annihilation. However, the price we pay for withholding information about who we are is loneliness. So, the risk is necessary. One good thing to keep in mind when revealing yourself is that your goal should be just that: self-revelation. If the focus is on the response, you are in danger of falling back into the manipulation pattern discussed in the previous chapter, in addition to placing yourself in the victim role.

Of course, you would like a positive response. Who doesn't? However, it should not be the goal. The goal is to know and be known in the inner self. As such, you are successful if you self-reveal, regardless of the response you receive. Fortunately, others are usually much more accepting of our deeper self than we are. They have faults and flaws too, and they not only admire the courage we show in revealing ourselves, but often feel honored that we chose to reveal ourselves to them.

Some years ago, a woman said to me, "I like you, David. I am not saying this so that you will like me back. I just wanted you to know that I like you."

That woman modeled perfectly what I am saying. She revealed to me what she was feeling, but did not in any way restrict my freedom to respond.

There is an added benefit in self-revealing without concern for the response. It is that people will usually like you better. Paradoxically, one of the laws of human behavior is that those who receive the most approval are those who seek it the least. Such people not only send out confident, attractive signals, but also are not manipulative and smothering of those with whom they share.

In any case, if you lack a stable sense of self-acceptance, the best advice I can give you about self-revelation is to take the risk. You may find the desensitization approach effective—opening up gradually to certain select people. It is almost never as bad as you anticipate it to be. Even if you don't get back exactly what you hope for, remember that others' responses can in no way lessen your value. Your value is a fixed commodity. You remain—after all—a valuable creation of God in his image. In addition, you can feel an enormous sense of accomplishment because you met your main objective: revealing something significant about yourself to another.

If you feel uneasy, you might want to begin by saying, "This is very difficult for me, because I am not used to talking about myself, but . . ." or, "I have to admit I am a bit nervous because I don't often speak so openly about who I am. . . ." These preparatory remarks will do wonders to put you at ease, because they remove the obligation of having to appear completely cool and in perfect control. And, you have already revealed something significant: you are neither cool, nor in control. Knowing that, the other person will find it easier to respond appropriately and you will have gotten rid of a good deal of your own anxiety.

Self-revelation, moving from hidden to open, is not the only way to open your Johari Window. You can also shrink the blind section. That involves feedback. Honest feedback is very important because it leads to deeper self-knowledge. It supplies us with valuable insights into ourselves. Frequently these insights are not flattering, since the material we do not know often involves matters we have repressed due to our disinclination to face them. However, the blind material is part of us, and even if it is negative, we cannot change and improve unless we know and accept what is in us.

Feedback almost always follows self-revelation. Others will withhold deep feelings they have about us, or intimate insights into our characters, until we demonstrate our openness by revealing something of significance.

Nevertheless, getting honest feedback is not automatic. You may have to ask for it. Really, there is nothing to fear, because almost without exception, others will admire your openness and do their feeding back with maximum tact and respect. If what they say is not all positive, you can still be grateful because, again, you can't change what you don't know. Besides, the measure of a friend is his honesty, not his unflagging shower of compliments.

One effective method to get feedback is to follow a self-revelation with, "What do you think of that?" If you are concerned about a friend being absolutely honest, tell him honesty is what you want. You might say, "If you want to be a good friend, tell me the absolute truth of what you think, rather than just something nice."

Feedback will often follow quite naturally if you have done some honest self-revealing. Feedback can be very important in removing Loneliness Out. Once people know you can stand up to the truth and value their opinion, their respect for you will grow. Most people are not looking for a flawless friend, just an authentic one. Welcoming honest responses is a demonstration of that authenticity.

The locked section gives way to a dual process of self-revelation and feedback. Think back to times when you have gotten into truly heavy raps about yourself with someone else. As you pried open the hidden parts of your character, they've responded with their observations of you. Then, by putting together your disclosures and their observations, together you stumbled onto new insights about yourself. What you did is break open *locked* material. In fact, a good therapist is in the business of helping you unlock material that is central to who you are. Such a therapist is certainly not a "shrink," he is a "stretch," working to expand your awareness.

We can't really leave the Johari Window without discussing one other important aspect of building intimacy. That is listening effectively.[6] You may have found yourself in situations in which someone is pouring out his soul and you just don't know what to say. Even worse, out of anxiety, you say the wrong thing; the person talking clams

93

up; and the conversation either ends abruptly or fades to a, "My, that is a nice stereo" level.

Before pointing out what you should do when listening to some intense material, let me mention a few "thou shalt nots." These involve very common intimacy killers which nearly everyone has engaged in.

Blaming a person for his feelings. "I'm so angry at my mother," screams Joan, "that I swear, if she mentions that issue one more time, I am going to tell her never to talk to me again! I just despise her for meddling!"

"Hey," Nancy says with calm innocence, "that's no way to feel about your mother. She means well, and after all, she does love you."

Instantly, Joan freezes up and changes the subject to a lighter topic.

What Joan wanted was not agreement or advice. Just an empathetic listening ear. Chances are Joan realized she was overstating the case, but she needed to vent her spleen and believed she was safe in doing so with Nancy. Once Nancy blamed Joan for her angry feelings, Joan felt unloved and uncared for. As far as she was concerned, despite Nancy's good intentions, she had received rejection instead of the unconditional love and acceptance she hoped to get in her moment of emotional vulnerability. So Joan decided inwardly that Nancy was not the person she wanted to be open with.

Explaining away feelings. "Tina and I have been married for two months," says Jerome, "and there are nights when I am so upset I want to run away and never come back."

"Don't worry, Jerome," Gary responds with the noblest of intentions, "every newly married couple finds those first few months of adjustment tough. It is a normal stage of marriage; even the best ones go through it."

Instead of finding someone who would participate in his pain and confusion, Jerome received a brief lecture—delivered personally and at no charge—on marital adjustment. If Jerome had wanted advice he would have written to Ann

Landers. What he wanted was a friend to bounce his feelings off of, in order to regain his perspective in going through that period of adjustment Gary had so articulately described.

Instant identification. "This is a really painful time for me," Barbara says. "My father is very ill and I don't know how long he will last."

"I know just how you feel," Jean blurts out, anxiously hurrying to the rescue. "Why, just last year my favorite uncle was at the brink of death. He pulled through, but that sure was rough on me."

Barbara doesn't care one whit about Jean's uncle last year. She is enmeshed in her own feelings about her father *now*. Jean's telling her how well she can identify communicates exactly the opposite message. It shows Jean hasn't identified at all. What Barbara wanted was for Jean to identify with her pain now—by listening fully, patiently, and caringly—not a report of a similar event in Jean's past.

Denying another's feelings. "Those gossips at the office are driving me nuts," Gina explodes. "I could kill them!"

"Come on, Gina," Mary says gently. "I know you better than that. You don't really feel that way."

Mary has just called Gina a liar. Though unintentional, that is what has happened, and Gina responds accordingly. She closes down.

As far as Gina is concerned, Mary is not really open to her inner pain, but is demeaning the intensity of her feelings by not taking them seriously. Indeed, Gina may at some level be aware that she is exaggerating her feelings. But it is up to Gina to acknowledge that. If she had wanted mind reading, she would have consulted a psychic. What Gina wanted was a release from the loneliness of her rage.

In every case, the listener did not mean to shut the person off. Or did he? Frequently, when we hear something painful we feel an indefinable sensation of anxiety inside. It is often a sign that we ourselves have pain and discomfort we haven't dealt with fully. When others open up some of theirs, we may find that, instead of receiving and processing it, we let it stimulate some of our own. The first emotional reflex is to quell this anxiety by shutting the other person off. Each of these reactions is a socially acceptable, although insensitive, way of doing so. It is a reflex in that we are often not conscious of our goal—to get away from the painful messages that are calling up some of our anxious stuff. It happens so fast, the words leave our mouth before we can think about what we are doing.

In the lion's share of cases, when people pour out their frustrations, anger, and disappointments, they are not looking for advice. They simply want a listener who cares. They want love to release them from the loneliness of their feelings. And love is listening with care. If they want advice, they will usually ask for it. However, if you have something really important to say, it is usually wise to wait until they are *completely* through with their catharsis. Until they have emptied their bucket fully, they neither want nor are able to listen to anything you say.

So often we pick up the wrong signals. We think they want advice, and so, instead of listening with love and care as they are talking, we sift through our gray matter for the "right words" to tell them. Not only does their anxiety evoke anxiety in us—we feel prevailed upon to deliver oracle-like wisdom.

Staying calm and keeping silent are the keys. Often I put my hand over my mouth when I listen to people so that I am physically reminded not to give in to my impulse to blurt out some crumb of advice. It seems that stifling myself is the best way to unstifle them.

MEETING NEW PEOPLE

Meeting new people can be difficult. We feel ill at ease, nervous, and so tend to avoid meeting others all together, settling for Loneliness Out.

Meeting others does not have to be that painful. There is

no reason why you have to feel you'll make a fool of yourself if you keep certain things in mind, particularly if you know the proper technique of self-presentation.

Meeting a new person—an encounter—usually has four parts: a greeting, response, content, and close.[7] The greeting is very important, because from it the other person will gain his first impression of you.

First impressions resist change. I learned that years ago when I met a rather famous author and critic, reputed to be one of the nicest people in the business. I called him about a book of mine, saying, "I am a humble author in this city, and I was wondering. . . ."

"There are no humble authors," he interrupted gruffly. "Get to your point."

He became more cordial as we spoke; and as it turned out, he liked my book, giving it a public endorsement which helped immeasurably. I had several later contacts with him in which he was very warm and friendly. Perhaps I had called him initially at the wrong time or on a bad day. However, it took a long time for me to feel good about him simply because of that stiff opening.

To make a good first impression, you want to send out the signals of being *relaxed* and *friendly*. There are several exercises you can use to reduce your nervousness. A preliminary one is to breathe deeply and slowly. Whenever you are nervous, the fight-or-flight syndrome swings into action, making your breathing short, rapid, and choppy. That alarm reaction heightens your anxiety. Slowing your body down by deep and slow inhaling and exhaling, as if you were a large balloon gradually filling and just as gradually emptying itself of air, will have a psychologically calming effect. Since you cannot be relaxed and anxious at the same time, this exercise will do wonders.

People like to be around relaxed, friendly people. So loosen your body language as well. Beginning with the top of your head, imagine water is falling on you, muscle by muscle, from your head to your feet, releasing the tension of each muscle it falls upon. As you relax the body muscles you will experience a soothing psychological effect. Also, as you meet a person, square your shoulders toward him so that your body is not in some fashion turned away. Turning suggests rejection and discomfort. When you shake his hand or say hello, move toward him a bit, telling him non-verbally that you really are welcoming him and are open to him.

As you ready yourself to talk, keep your throat open. Yawning without opening your mouth is a good method. It opens your throat and will prevent that tight, squeaky sound which reeks of nervousness. When you do speak, speak slowly and pleasantly. The key mental tip is to try to help the other person relax. If you concentrate on contributing to the other's relaxation you will feel relaxed yourself. You will be so busy concentrating on helping the other person feel good, you will have no opportunity to feel self-conscious.

As for being friendly, smile. People like to see others smile at them. There are so many grim and angry faces to look at as we trudge to and from our appointed rounds that a warm and smiling face is a very welcome sight. Smiling tells others you like them and are pleased to meet them. Everyone likes to be liked, so smile. If you have difficulty with this, practice everything from extending your hand for a firm but pleasant handshake to flashing a warm smile in front of a mirror.

The second part of an encounter is a response—the other person's first reaction. Watch closely for both verbal and nonverbal cues. If the other person is warm and friendly, with open body language, you are off to a good start. If he seems rather stiff, loosen your muscles even more to help him feel more at ease. If he seems preoccupied, or in a hurry, make your greeting brief and get back to him later if possible. In most cases, however, if you radiate relaxation and friendliness, you will get the same in return. The key to the response phase is keen observation on your part for cues to know where to go from there.

The content refers to what you will talk about as you move beyond the greeting and response stages. Here it is important to shift away from "It sure is a nice get together" small talk to something more substantial. Ask people personal things—about hobbies, advice, where they were born, where they live, whether they like their job, etc. People feel good when others show personal interest in them. There are a host of things you can ask another person which focus on him specifically, but are not violations of privacy. Move in that direction so that both of you feel you have truly gotten acquainted.

The last part is the close. If you are with a member of the opposite sex you hope to see again, leave with a smile and say, "I really enjoyed meeting you; I hope to see you again." If he seems genuine in returning the compliment, and you are likely to be in the same place again, you may have a budding friendship or romance. If there is little certainty of your paths crossing in the future, move right into an, "I don't know that I am likely to see you again, so if you'll give me a number so I can call you, I'll get back to you." If you are reluctant to do that (many people are), tell the person where you work and that you hope you will see him again. At least he knows where you are much of the time and perhaps he will tell you where he works or where he can be located in return.

Though shyness is common, there is no need for it. Most people like to meet others. If you are friendly, they will want to see you again too. So consider being a bit more bold in trying to get a phone number.

The number one thing which prevents people from meeting others is fear of rejection. This is an irrational fear. It is irrational because upon first meeting someone you have not given him enough information about yourself for him to reject you in any meaningful way. The conversation has been so brief and superficial that nothing of real substance has been communicated so that valid rejection could take place.

Moreover, if the other person doesn't seem interested in you, there could be myriad reasons why, which have absolutely nothing to do with you. For example, he may be preoccupied with something else so that he just doesn't have the mental space to talk with anyone; he may be in a hurry and not want to bog himself down with meeting someone; he may be in a less than sociable mood at the moment and therefore closed to you; or something about you or your appearance may remind him of someone else in his past with whom he had a bad experience. In the case of a man-woman encounter, he may have someone else in his life and so is avoiding any other relationships. The list is endless, but the point is the same. If someone does not seem interested when meeting you, don't take it personally. The first thought you should have is, "What is *he* feeling?" Not, "What is wrong with *me?*"

There is nothing that helps overcome irrational fears of rejection as much as practice. That's right, go out there and meet as many people as you can—even people you are not very interested in—just to get over initial fears. If you need to use desensitization, do so. At first, pick only people you know are particularly gracious and charming, who will give you some good responses immediately. And from there, venture out. You will be on your way to kissing Loneliness Out good-bye. If you wonder where to go to meet people, see Figure 3.

ALONE BUT NOT LONELY

Despite all the opportunities to meet and form relationships, there are times when others are not available. That is when we feel Loneliness Out most acutely and need to know how to deal with it effectively.

One technique is to turn the negative feelings of Loneliness Out into a positive experience: solitude. Solitude is a time when we can transcend our daily worries, a positive time, a time for reflection, integration, and prayer.[8] Solitude is time alone with yourself, when you get into who you really are, what your relationship with yourself and God is. Christ spent much of his time going off alone to pray and fellowship with the Father. He looked forward to those times, planning to include them. They rebuilt and nourished his spirit.

Many Christians speak of their "quiet time." It is a time spent away from others and the mind-numbing outside world; time which is used in reading Scripture, praying, and thinking. This is what solitude is. Out of it comes a deeper knowledge and acceptance of our own self as well as learning how to take care of yourself. In addition, it removes the terror of being alone, with the peace of knowing that being alone can be an enriching experience.

One good way to break that loneliness terror with solitude is to schedule some time alone every day. At first, it may seem awkward, even difficult, with vestiges of loneliness creeping into your awareness. However, if you stay with it—thinking, reading, praying, reflecting—you will soon come to value that time and no longer fear other moments when there is no one around to be with.

Meditation is a very effective form of solitude. There is no need to use an eastern word as a mantra to gain its benefits. You can use a word such as "Jesus," or "peace." In any case, lie down in as relaxed a position as possible, and repeat the word softly and slowly for ten to twenty minutes daily. Empty your mind of all competing thoughts as you enter an inner world with which you are unfamiliar, but one which is an important part of you. If, as you meditate, other thoughts crowd in, simply say, "No," and refocus on your meditating word. Again, at first you will fade in and out in your meditation; but as you make it a habit it will be one of the most treasured parts of your day—alone.

Solitude is much more than learning how to be alone

without feeling lonely. It is necessary for rebuilding your inner life. Out of that practice you will become more comfortable with yourself in every way. You will learn how to turn moments alone into positive experiences, and you will truly learn how to be your own best friend.

You can learn to live much closer to God in your moments of solitude. You can listen rather than simply talk to God. The peace of that solitude must be experienced. It cannot be described. But the strength and quiet power derived from it are not available anywhere else.

If you find solitude difficult to get into, there are books on meditation and prayer which can be very helpful. Browsing through a religious or mainline bookstore, finding something you feel comfortable with, and then following its instructions can get you on your way.

Writing can also help you be alone without being lonely. Through the most difficult periods of my life I kept a personal journal. Daily, I recorded the feelings going on inside of me. It was an enormously liberating experience as I poured my inner loneliness out onto the pages, feeling delivered from much of it as I wrote. In addition, I was able to chart growth in myself and my faith as the days passed and I reviewed what I had written. I felt a newer and deeper inner strength of faith and character which was exhilarating. I realized I was not only surviving being alone, I was growing and developing.

If you have a poetic gift, use it. It can be very therapeutic. It is a way of emptying your soul of the feelings lodged inside, turning pain into beauty and confusion into truth. If you have never written poetry before, try it. You may discover not only a gift you didn't realize you had, but an enormous inner satisfaction. Moreover, journal and poetry writing can be an excellent basis for reflection and prayer.

Rational reflection is also beneficial.[9] This is a time when you practice out loud talking with yourself rationally about feelings and problems that trouble you. At first, rational reflection will be difficult. Your mind will wander. You will stop talking out loud, finding yourself conversing inwardly in less than full, clear, and rational sentences. Your feelings will get in the way, and it will be hard to concentrate on one issue and see it through. However, you will become better at it the more you do it. Over time, you will learn how to give yourself very good, practical, and rational advice. Again, you will become your own best and most respected friend.

As you employ rational reflection more regularly, you will trust your own thinking more and will break the habit many lonely people fall into—constantly calling their friends for advice. It also undercuts the loneliness tendency toward impulsive behavior, discussed earlier.

In the spirit of rational reflection, Edgar Jackson offers a creative idea.[10] He suggests developing a mental committee of true friends, people you respect who can nurture your spirit. This committee is always present for discussion and consultation so that you are never really alone.

Committee members can be living or dead, from this era or centuries past. Also, you can change or add members at any time. Jackson's committee was composed of Socrates, who could ask the depth question in a search for truth; St. Francis, who modeled openness, love, and warmth toward all living things; John Wesley, a man of incredible intelligence and energy, whose influence changed English culture and religious life; Thoreau, who transcended material concern as he communed with nature; Simone Weil, who showed how to put God first in her life of devotion to his purposes; and Paul Robeson, whose courage in fighting for the oppressed, coupled with his great musical and dramatic talents, set him apart.

Such a mental committee has many values. It will give you a fuller and deeper perspective on life. It is creative in that you can draw from the written resources of these people. And it is available twenty-four hours a day.

The committee idea involves imagination—fantasy. Fantasizing is not only for children. Developing a rich fantasy life is enormously rewarding. Imagining you are some great figure from the past or newsmaker of today is fun and healthy. It can bring relief and give you a psychological vacation for the period during which you engage in fantasizing that you are that person. It also widens your perspective, getting you out of the narrow circle of your own loneliness, and enables you to learn a great deal about life by putting you in the position of others.

Returning to the world of others, involving yourself with lonely people, can be very liberating. Visiting the sick in your church or hospitals; volunteering at Christian or social agencies which need help; working with shut-ins or people in prison; or helping those who are elderly and alone can be immensely rewarding.

Giving some of your time to these causes does many things. It gets you moving and away from stagnating in your loneliness and brings the joy of helping others in a truly meaningful way. It also helps you see that you are not alone in your loneliness, but that in fact there are many people with greater problems than you. If you are a shut-in, simply phoning others in need will give you many of the same benefits.

One good way to overcome the fear of loneliness is to live alone. That's right. Look loneliness right in the face and challenge it by living by yourself. This may not work for everyone, but for those who have intense fears of being alone, diving in and finding out you will not die is a breakthrough.

LIVING NOW

Also, keep a focus on living *now*. Lying around hoping for something to happen next week, next month, or next year, is self-defeating. Make each day count. In fact, schedule each day as fully as you can with activities you want or need to do. Live in the now at every opportunity. Waiting alone brings on loneliness. If the ship of your hopes doesn't come in, you are setting yourself up for depression. So visit your friend now; go out to lunch today; catch that event you wanted to see tonight. Join that health club or exercise group immediately; don't sleep in on Sunday morning when you could go to church and see people you know.

Be especially careful to schedule your weekends. Don't let a weekend come without a plan of some sort. Take on a part-time job, volunteer your time at a hospital or church, make certain you go to a social event you know is coming up. Plan for it. Dead time on the weekend or hours spent pining away hoping for a breakthrough in the future are the stuff of loneliness. Waiting fosters that feeling of being on "hold" in the business of living while the rest of the world is moving.

So get moving, and move Loneliness Out *out*.

Figure 3.

Some places where women can meet men	Some places where men can meet women	Places where you can meet either sex
sports events	cooking classes	laundromats
self-defense classes	art classes	work
auto mechanics classes	exercise classes	luncheons
career classes	women's political	restaurants
active sports classes	functions	parties
business functions	supermarkets	churches
jogging	amusement parks	planes, trains, buses,
church activities	fashion shows	and taxis
		shopping centers
		public events
		museums
		movies
		plays
		public lectures

These are just idea starters. Check out women's and men's magazines and newspaper sections to get additional ideas of events and activities where you can meet someone.

CHAPTER 4

[1]An excellent source for dealing with the broken heart syndrome and its stages is *Letting Go,* by Dr. Zev Wanderer and Tracy Cabot (New York: Warner Books, 1978); also helpful is *How to Survive the Loss of a Love,* by Melba Colgrove, Harold H. Bloomfield, and Peter McWilliams (New York: Bantam Books, 1976).

[2]The following personality types are derived from *Why Am I Afraid to Tell You Who I Am?* by John Powell, S.J. (Niles, Ill.: Argus Communications, 1969), pp. 121–167. Powell gives pointed illustrations of self-defeating ways of relating as well as positive directions in his book.

[3]Daniel Goldstine, Katherine Larner, Shirley Zuckerman, and Hilary Goldstine, *The Dance-Away Lover* (New York: Ballantine Books, 1981), pp. 149–242.

[4]Lecture given by Dr. Wayne W. Dyer at North Park College, Chicago, Illinois, April 1982.

[5]The Johari Window and related figures are derived from Joseph Luft, *Group Processes* (Palo Alto, Calif.: National Press Books, 1970), pp. 11–21.

[6]The material on poor listening patterns is from a presentation by Dr. Em Griffin of Wheaton College given at LaSalle Street Church, Chicago, Illinois, May 18, 1975.

[7]Unpublished research by David Claerbaut for "Fifty Ways to Meet Your Lover," class sponsored by Chicago Alternatives, Chicago, Illinois.

[8]Terri Schultz, *Bittersweet* (New York: Penguin Books, 1978), p. 180.

[9]Robert J. Ringer, *Looking Out for #1* (New York: Fawcett Crest Books, 1977), pp. 137, 138.

[10]Edgar N. Jackson, *Understanding Loneliness* (Philadelphia: Fortress Press, 1981), pp. 135, 136.

5

INTRAPSYCHIC LONELINESS

Intrapsychic loneliness is loneliness within the self, a feeling of being out of harmony, separated, or alienated from one's self. There are a variety of causes of intrapsychic loneliness. However, two of the main ones are identity diffusion and low self-esteem.

IDENTITY DIFFUSION

Identity diffusion is a fancy way of saying that a person doesn't really have a clear picture of who he is. Although identity diffusion is a normal stage through which adolescents pass, it afflicts many adults as well. It brings with it a restlessness and anxiety which is hard to pin down. For adults, identity diffusion is dangerous because adulthood is a stage in which major decisions, from the choice of a spouse to the selection of a career, are made. When such decisions are entered into without a whole, integrated identity, terrible mistakes can result.

There are a number of forces that produce identity diffusion. One of them is sheer busyness. The pace of life is so intense that we are defined more by our roles than our personalities. People do not have opportunities to get to know us as persons, only as housewives, stenographers, professors, or plumbers. For the individual, this means precious little time to sit down, reflect, and come to know himself at length—little solitude.

I see high-powered professional people every day who are carrying great responsibility, possess great power, and enjoy immense prestige. However, after talking with them in depth they prove to be very superficial, living for immediate gratification and vague, long-term pleasure. They do not have a clear sense of the contours of their own psyche. They know everything about marketing international products, but nothing of themselves.

Armstrong's citing of the study which showed most subjects had no ultimate values at all touches this issue. In fact, identity is so closely tied to values—in many respects we *are* our values, what we live for and are committed to. Thus, living in a pleasure-saturated, value-drained culture makes identity formation difficult. A person without values is a person without direction. It is a person going nowhere.

A number of the forces mentioned in chapter 1 also contribute to identity diffusion. Among them is the proliferation of life options. There are so many choices available—from life style to occupation, residence to social life—it is difficult to choose.

Jerry had an IQ of 140. After cruising through college with a mediocre grade point average and minimal effort, he took a job as an orderly in a psychiatric hospital. The only profession that remotely appealed to Jerry was that of physician, but he didn't want it badly enough to prepare for medical school.

By the time he was thirty, Jerry had held about ten different jobs, from bartending to working in an employment agency. He was no closer to a settled occupational identity than he was at twenty-two. Very handsome, he had a harem of female acquaintances during those years. However, no one seemed right for him either. Jerry had no real defined values, no direction or goal. Without a direction, a goal, Jerry found it impossible to put down psychological roots, to gain depth. He, like so many others, reached widely but not deeply.

Whereas Jerry couldn't find anything he really wanted to do, Darlene, a very attractive young suburbanite, wanted to do everything. Darlene wanted to go to college, open a cosmetics business, get married, and enter broadcast journalism. Without knowing what to do, Darlene sat, as though on a lazy susan, observing the array of life choices passing her by.

Indeed, for many of us, we are what we do. Our occupation is central to how we perceive ourselves. The reality of this occupationally centered identity is driven home each time we meet someone new. When I introduce myself saying, "Hi, I'm Dr. Claerbaut. I teach sociology and psychology," I can be certain of two things: (1) people will forget my name immediately; and (2) they will remember that I am a professor. As far as they are concerned, I *am* what I do.

However, even this occupational identity is not completely secure. In a shifting economy—filled with career changes and losses, as well as altered job descriptions— occupational identity is no longer as simple and certain as being the town barber. Hence, it is one less thing to hold on to in fixing our identity.

Constant residential mobility and the resulting rootlessness are also problematic. Once you move out of the community in which you were reared, you have discarded much of who you were in the lives of others. You are no longer an Elm Grover, but are now a suburban New Yorker —whatever that is.

Friends and family who were meaningful in your development (your becoming who you are) leave the scene and no longer play important roles in your identity. Moreover, new people, whom you didn't know before, take over.

Even marriage does not always secure familial identity. In the past, when your spouse almost certainly came from the same community as you, marriage put you in a more established context. Not so anymore. Joe grew up in a small midwestern town. His was a strict Christian upbringing by parents who held tightly to a very traditional male-dominated marriage style. Joe never saw his parents either show intense affection or fight. He lived in an Ozzie and Harriet world, one in which smiles predominated and conflict did not exist. In college, he met Renee, who came from a broken home in a large eastern city. Having common religious beliefs while meeting certain deficits in one another's personalities, Joe and Renee got married six months later.

It didn't work. Brought up in totally different backgrounds, Joe's idea of the roles of husband and wife varied sharply from that of Renee. While Joe feared conflict, suppressing it with an authoritarian style, Renee felt squelched. They were divorced in four years.

Joe and Renee's tragedy reminds us that in today's society, your spouse may come from a different part of the country, or even world, and therefore from a radically different background than yours. Despite our desire for two to become one, marriage can develop into a series of painful compromises and even rather regular but disconcerting switches back and forth from one spouse's world to the other's.

One of the biggest contributors to identity diffusion, however, is the lack of personal relationships. It is the personal relationship that most strongly reinforces our uniqueness, celebrating those aspects that differentiate us from everyone else. Those relationships help us feel comfortable digging into our personality, finding what is at the root.

However, impersonal relationships, which dominate in an urban culture, place us in general categories, making us very similar to thousands of others. We are that young person, that graduate student, that black schoolteacher, that hairdresser—hardly unique designations. The more of these relationships we have, the more we feel we are really no different from millions of others; and hence, not really unique enough to be missed if we were gone. Self-worth suffers.

We first are introduced to this impersonal atmosphere in school. There we confront formal instructions, learning which is designed to devclop our intellectual capacities.[1] There is an attempt to stay away from values and personal growth, as everything is focused in the direction of what is objective and scientific. The school operates as though values are unimportant.

Accentuating this formula for identity diffusion is the emphasis on competition rather than cooperation.[2] Students compete for awards, attention, positions on the football team and cheerleading squad, roles in the play, and grades. The competition separates them. It does not provide them with a harmonious environment in which they can help one another learn who they really are. Instead of a relaxed atmosphere in which personalities can develop and be discovered, there is a frantic, busy environment in which students scramble for rewards.

The occupational world is becoming increasingly scientific and impersonal. As Tournier points out, "Science itself depersonalizes man."[3] It attempts to "eliminate the individual factor, the personal coefficient, and to repress everything that stirred up his [the person's] heart."[4]

For many, this divests work of all personal meaning. It cuts a human's occupational effort away from his values. Moreover, with everything being objective and scientific— even worse, highly competitive—it undercuts the growth of truly personal relationships.

In my work with major league baseball players, I find very few personal relationships. Although they are members of a team, such that one would think there would be a sense of unity, they are not only competing with members of other teams, but with one another for security on their own teams. This situation, in addition to the fact that they may be traded or released at any time, discourages them from ever getting close to a fellow player. Many of them are very lonely and confused.

The research indicates that senior citizens and suburban housewives often have acute identity problems. On the surface, these two groups would seem to have little in common. Upon closer look, however, we find that they share one key characteristic: social isolation. The elderly live in a world devoid of meaningful relationships, imprisoned in apartments or nursing homes. The suburban housewife is often held hostage in a world of children, with few peers who can nourish her uniqueness and identity.

Phyllis, thirty, was married with two small children. At first she enjoyed the life of a homemaker, and was excited as she watched her children grow. As the years passed, she became increasingly bored. The children became an annoyance, her hobbies were few, and time with her tired husband scarce. Starving for personal relationships and feeling as if her life was racing away, she had an affair which ended her marriage. She was scorned in her community, as people contrasted Phyllis' affair with her hard-working husband's faithfulness. Yet she remained brazen, rationalizing that the finger-pointing townsfolk could never understand the social "isolation booth" she had lived in. Phyllis' behavior was self-defeating and harmful to people she loved; however, it does highlight the lengths to which people will go when thirsting for a personal relationship.

Through all this, the media doesn't help us much either. It spews forth oceans of competing value systems, leaving us confused over what to believe or how to live. In addition, radio, TV, and magazines are passive forms of entertainment. So, instead of developing our identities, we sit exposed to two-dimensional people, mountains of controversy, and a steady stream of unrealistic presentations of life. For those devoid of personal relationships, the Disneyland world which the media presents can invade one's sense of reality and responsible living.

Perhaps the greatest cause of identity diffusion is what I

call the "external personality."[5] Externals are people who see only a limited relationship between what they do and what happens to them. They look to outside forces for cues to determine what action to take; and, more importantly, they attribute how they feel to external conditions.

Grammatically speaking, externals place themselves in the object phase of a sentence. For example, "You make me feel..." and, "It makes me think..." are external statements. Because we think in words, words like these tip you off that a person is looking outside himself for explanations of his behavior and feelings.

Externals are in the majority. It has been said that three fourths of the American society is external.[6] There are a number of reasons for this.

For openers, it's easier. Being external enables us to blame society, our parents, other people, God, the weather, "the breaks," or any other convenient outside force for life's disappointments.

Listen to students. "I got an A," one proclaims loudly. "I got a B+," says another. "I made it too," sighs a relieved student. "I got a C." The unsuccessful student? *"He gave me a D,"* he grumbles bitterly.

We live in a Rodney Dangerfield, "I can't get no respect," culture. Everything out there—from commercials which tell us a certain product will *make* us desirable, to many psychological therapies which teach us how to blame our parents rather than change our lives—encourages external thinking.

The external is a high risk for intrapsychic loneliness; whereas internals—those who see a strong relationship between what they do and what happens to them—develop their identity through self-direction. They take responsibility for their own life and choices.

Externals look to the outside—from others to the media —for what to do, how to act, and who to be. With a myriad of models—from rock idols to famous Christians— it is little wonder that the external's self-image soon becomes an uneasy hodge-podge of people he allows to impress him.

An additional problem is that that hodge-podge doesn't even stay in place. As one model fades and is no longer stylish, another takes its place. Confusion sets in as identity diffusion becomes permanent.

This doesn't happen only with adolescents. Jeff is a terminal external. In college during the 60s, Jeff was impressed by the "Big Man on Campus" image. So he went about becoming the Campus Clothes Horse. After a year of high-profile, partygoing social elitism, Jeff noticed that the more well known intellectual students were not impressed.

The next fall Jeff adopted the scholar role. Attired in grubby blue jeans, he grew a beard, enrolled in philosophy courses, and developed a very academic vocabulary. By the time he graduated, Jeff had turned into a social activist. He got married and entered social work.

Ten years later I ran into Jeff at a major college basketball game in another city. Divorced, he was living with a woman and pursuing the dream of becoming an actor. Today I occasionally see Jeff in television commercials, but Hollywood is a long way off and the commercials are few and far between for Jeff. He is making most of his money painting houses.

Jeff's life is a poignant illustration that if one's identity does not get developed, brick by brick, through responsible, mature, self-directed behavior, identity diffusion will remain well into adulthood.

Erikson suggests that people like this are never able to take hold of their own lives, but like Jeff, live in shifting psychological sand.[7]

It is a painful place to be.

WHAT TO DO

The first thing to do is realize that your identity is not a given, it is developed. You build and expand it.

It begins with self-knowledge. This can't be taken for granted. People are often not aware of their own feelings. Eugene O'Neill, in his famous play, *The Ice Man Cometh,* tells the story of Hickey, who, after creating a miserable marital environment with his drinking, murders his hated wife. Unable to accept the guilt associated with his hateful feelings, Hickey tries—with limited success—to rationalize his actions.

> So I killed her. (There is a moment of dead silence.) And then I saw I'd always known that was the only possible way to give her peace and free her from the misery of loving me. I saw it meant peace for me, too, knowing she was at peace. I felt at though a ton of guilt was lifted off my head. I remember I stood by the bed and suddenly I had to laugh. I couldn't help it, and I knew Evelyn would forgive me. I remember I heard myself speaking to her, as if it was something I'd always wanted to say: "Well, you know what you can do with your pipe dream now...."[8]

What Hickey did was repress feelings he could not face squarely. Christians have, I believe, a particular problem with repression. We are so conditioned to feel guilty about sin because of our awareness of our flawed natures that our minds do not want to confront the common feelings of hate, resentment, jealousy, dissatisfaction, lust, and anger. However, we cannot know who we are unless we own our feelings—all of them.

So, an initial step is to let yourself feel your feelings. Feelings are not you. They are part of you. In many cases, they pass through you like clouds through the sky on a summer day. Realizing that, don't shut them off.

This may take practice. Professor Felton was a highly esteemed theologian. Much of his popularity owed to his gentle, loving spirit. Those who knew him well, however, noticed one thing that disturbed them. Professor Felton never got angry—about anything. In fact, instances occurred which should have elicited anger, but the professor didn't become angry—ever. In fact, he never showed any intense emotion. When those around him did, he became uncomfortable.

Professor Felton did have feelings. He was, after all, a mortal with all the flaws of the rest of us. His problem was that he felt guilty about negative emotions—so negative that he had what I call an emotional bypass. As soon as his psyche detected the slightest tremor of anger, resentment, or any other less than noble emotion, it was shifted through the bypass, which neutralized it with a calm, I'm-not-upset humility. Hence, the guilt, which automatically accompanied any of his assertive, hostile feelings and thoughts, would be assuaged.

People brought up in homes where anger and hostility are unpardonable often develop these bypasses in order to survive. They need to handle the negative emotions somehow without triggering guilt. We have to be careful here, however. We need not condemn Professor Felton for his self-control. Developing emotional control is a sign of maturity and growth. What is at stake here is his denial of the emotion itself, for fear of it.

Feeling your feelings is vital in knowing what is inside you. In terms of right and wrong, the feeling is not the issue. What you *do* with it is. However, feelings must be acknowledged. You cannot change them unless you first accept them for what they are.

The value of experiencing your feelings is that it has a cleansing effect. It empties your soul of hidden hostilities and resentments which have been simmering there. If you find, as you acknowledge more immediately what you feel, that certain feelings are particularly common, then pay attention to them. Such feelings constitute personality characteristics. They are a part of who you are on a consistent basis.

If you have trouble with acknowledging your feelings—

even to yourself—you might try this exercise. Any time you feel something you sense a desire to suppress, deny, or be ashamed of, repeat to yourself the previously mentioned statement three times: "I have a right to my feelings." You do. You are not saying you are happy with those feelings, proud of them, or intend to act according to them. Just that they are yours and you have a right to them. In any case, dig into the ground of your feelings. I don't know of any person who has a good sense of who he is *without* a good grip on what he feels.

Opening up to another on a consistent basis is also helpful. This docs not have to be a therapist, although one may help. James urges us to confess our sins to each other (5:16). This must be the most overlooked verse in the entire Bible. But it is so practical. Opening your emotions to a friend— uncensored, unedited, and unvarnished—is an excellent way to find out what is inside and how to understand and control it.

Do the same in your prayer life. Many believers have trouble with emotional outpourings to God. They are so bogged down in "Thees," "Thous," and other traditional expressions that the idea of telling God how enraged they are has never occurred to them.

Tell him. He knows already and I'm sure he's able to handle it. In fact, he can't help you handle it unless you confess it.

Friends also can help by feeding back what they observe in you. Listen carefully because they often see things you don't, or, like Hickey, your mind doesn't want you to see. But it can be invaluable in learning what is ticking inside your brain.

Once you get a sense of what your emotional machinery is like, you have made a great step forward. Now trace those feelings back to your thoughts. That's right. Feelings come from thoughts. The book of Proverbs isn't kidding when it says, "As a man thinks, so he is."

Feelings are physiological responses to thoughts. If you

doubt that, consider that if your brain were damaged so that you could not think, you would also have no feelings. Whenever you feel anything, you receive a message, perhaps extremely brief and instantaneous, from your cognitive (thinking) system.

So trace your feelings backward to your thoughts. What thoughts trigger off rage? What do you think for that split-second prior to feeling resentful? Look closely; think it through carefully. You may not be able to uncover the actual thoughts immediately because the mind can be deceitful, especially when it harbors something we don't feel good about. But be assured, it is there.

Once you sink your teeth into what those thoughts are, you know a great deal more about who you are and what motivates you. And once you know what the feelings, and then the thoughts, are, you are in a new position—one in which you are able to gain control of those feelings and change.

There are other methods available to gain self-knowledge and so reduce intrapsychic loneliness. Keeping an identity journal is very useful. It is similar to the journal discussed in the previous chapter, but in it you write briefly, daily, things which you discover about yourself. Just keeping a journal will help you tune in more carefully throughout the day to who you are. Writing out feelings, thoughts, and insights helps you gain a better grip, a stronger and more vivid awareness of what's inside. It also charts growth—growth in self-knowledge and growth in changing to become the person you want to be.

Don't neglect the journal. Write something in it every day, even if it is a reiteration of what you've discovered previously. You can also use it to schedule new confrontations with self-discovery. Lyle did this in charting his feelings about a young woman he had fallen deeply in love with a year previously. He hadn't seen her since the relationship had ended and thought he might be over it. Not certain, he decided to put it to the test.

He determined to go to her apartment when he knew she would be home and say, "Hello." He would do no more. Definitely nothing to effect a continuation of their relationship. But simply seeing her, he would be able to tell, when he left, whether he was over her. If the aftermath of seeing her was painful, he knew he was still "hung-up." He chose this, and was willing to face the consequences. Fortunately, the rendezvous was civil and friendly, and Lyle left knowing he still cared but was no longer under the power of the relationship.

A good time to write in your journal is during periods of planned solitude. In the last chapter, we talked at great length of the value of solitude in dispelling Loneliness Out. It is every bit as helpful in dealing with Intrapsychic Loneliness. Listening to yourself, your thoughts and feelings, without distraction is an excellent way not only to get acquainted with who you are, but also to become more comfortable with yourself. The more comfortable you become with who you are, the more able you will be to hear what is going on inside. It is cyclical. Knowledge brings comfort, and comfort enables you to relax and gain additional knowledge.

It has to *start* somewhere. Solitude is the place. Daily. This can include prayer, meditation, rational reflection, Scripture reading, or journal writing. But at some time during your period of solitude, perhaps twenty to forty minutes daily, you need to listen to yourself carefully and quietly and think about what you hear.

There is another short exercise you may find effective in working at identity sharpening. Have someone sit down with you and ask, "Who are you?" Respond with only a sentence or two, after which your partner repeats the question. Do this question and response repetition for five minutes. This can be a very helpful technique, because after the first few minutes, all the superficial material will be used up, and more significant things will emerge.

When using this method, it is important, however, to follow three ground rules. First, do not make eye contact with your partner. This avoids distracting self-consciousness. Also, do not expand on any responses. Make them brief so that you retain your focus and time is not wasted. You can probe your responses more deeply later. Finally, do not have your partner comment at any time during the exercise. His only activity is to repeat the question *slowly,* after every response.

If you want to get more directly at values, you can use other questions, such as, "What do you want?" or the sentence completion technique, "I value. . . ." Moreover, although it is helpful to have a partner ask the trigger question, you can do this exercise alone, by repeating the question to yourself after each brief response. If you do it alone, it is wise to tape the exercise. Under any circumstances, use a time limit (five minutes is about right) to discipline your concentration.

Out of these various exercises will emerge your values— what you are committed to. That, as we said earlier, is central to your identity. Indeed, "Where your treasure is, there will your heart be also" (Matthew 6:21).[9] The heart is your identity. So, if you want to know where your heart is, find what you treasure—your values.

Again, your values may not be things you are proud of. You may not like some of the things that truly turn you on. However, before you can change them, you have to know what they are.

As you reflect, write, and discover, you will also determine what values you are going to embrace. For Christians who read Scripture carefully and thoughtfully, there is much direction in value formation. So, you will not only be discovering your values, but also forming and determining them. In any case, no search for identity is complete without values clarification, because it is those values which tell you where you are going.

LOW SELF-ESTEEM

The other contributor to Intrapsychic Loneliness is low self-esteem. There is no overestimating the importance of your self-image. How you see yourself is the single most important psychological determinant in your life. You behave in accordance with your self-image. If you feel you are a winner, you will act in winning ways. If you see yourself as a failure, you will give up easily and accept defeat. If you feel confident, you act confidently. If you feel inferior, you tend to act self-effacingly.

Moreover, our self-concepts are reflected. They are based on how we feel others (most importantly our parents) see us. This is very helpful to keep in mind, because it gives you a very good hint as to how you came to feel the way you do about yourself. You know where and at whom to look in determining what messages you receive about yourself, material that influences how you see yourself.

Bill is a very likable twenty-seven-year-old young man. Yet he has no success with women, can't hold a job, and feels like a failure. You need look no further than Bill's mother to see how Bill came to feel so negatively about himself and act in accordance with that feeling. Bill's father, who was very accepting of him, died when he was young. His mother is a very bitter and frustrated woman. Her main domestic activity was to complain to Bill about his behavior, telling him he would "never amount to anything." Bill has heard these put-down messages his entire life. In fact, once when he was a child, he was not allowed to sit with his friends or eat any cake at his own birthday party.

The effect of these messages in this bizarre environment has been for Bill to feel he cannot do anything right. So he has difficulty even trying. Bill is very passive and unable—unless strongly provoked—to express any assertiveness.

Bill is an extreme case, but all of us can learn from him in determining how we came to feel the way we do about ourselves. Moreover, parents do more than simply tell us what we are like and what we are worth. They also model how

121

we are to feel about ourselves. Parents with very depressed self-images, suffering from a "such-a-worm-as-I" theology of self-rejection, teach their children how to hate and reject themselves through a false humility.

Brothers and sisters, childhood friends, and other significant figures in our past also contribute. Margie, a senior citizen, is a hostile and depressed woman. Though she felt loved by her parents, Margie's older sister constantly fought her for attention, and in the process tried to put Margie down as an unwelcome competitor. To this day, Margie has an abnormal need for recognition, and smolders with silent hostility if she doesn't receive what she feels she merits. Instead of feeling confident and secure about herself, she needs others to tell her she is important and worthwhile, as if her sister were still there to steal attention from her.

Whenever you don't feel good about yourself, you are bound to be lonely within. The reason for this inner alienation is that people who have low self-esteem are constantly on the run from themselves. They are estranged and alienated from who they are as certainly as they are estranged and alienated from others.

Jack had no concept of who he was. His relationship with his parents, friends, and women—all were in trouble. The more I probed Jack, the more I realized that he was deeply uncomfortable with who he was. He stayed frantically busy, from the moment he arose to the time he went to bed, with activities involving other people. This enabled Jack to avoid sitting down and facing who he was.

I gave Jack one assignment. I told him to spend a certain amount of time each week alone, thinking about and getting to know himself. He found the assignment too difficult. Jack's self-esteem was so low, that getting to know who he was was too painful. He'd rather run, remaining an intrapsychically lonely person—a fugitive from his own identity.

The first step in improving your self-esteem is to make a

decision to face yourself as you are. It's no different from "facing off" with your feelings and values; you must forsake Jack's style and look into the psychological mirror.

Once you have stared deeply into that mirror, you have to accept what's there. Self-acceptance, something we discussed briefly earlier, is basic to developing self-esteem.

It is important to remember that self-acceptance does not imply a self-love of a narcissistic, self-centered sort. Instead, it means that you accept—face up to—yourself for who you are, with minuses as well as pluses. Self-acceptance means you are not going to punish yourself, reject yourself, deny who you are, or nag yourself. You are going to accept, take responsibility for, and nurture yourself.

You cannot repair your car if you reject it by beating it with a tire iron. Similarly, you cannot become the person you want to be, if you condemn and castigate yourself. You don't improve anything by destroying and damaging it—least of all, your own self-image.

If a friend of yours were sick, you probably would accept him, taking care of and nurturing him to recovery. You would not abuse him and attack him because of his physical afflictions. Yet, when our self-concept is one which suggests that we are not what we want to be, we turn on ourselves, railing and raging away at our imperfections, making ourselves feel even worse. And of course, that feeling of depressed self-rejection drains us of the energy necessary for improvement.

Once you decide to accept yourself for who you are, you are ready for a venture out of irrational thinking into clear, logical self-assessment. That's right; most people's poor self-esteem is due to irrational thinking. They have fallen into patterns of thinking which guarantee one internal putdown after another until they come to hate themselves. In fact, this tendency toward using thought distortions is so common, we can outline five of the most common ones that help people feel bad about themselves. The five thought distortions we will discuss are adapted from *Feeling Good,* an insightful book which deals with thinking rationally. If you suffer from a poor self-concept, I can almost guarantee that you are a master at using one or more of these thought distortions.[10]

Either/or thinking.[11] Either/or thinking holds that there is nothing between the extremes of good and bad, right and wrong, success and failure. Either/or people tend to have perfectionist standards so that whenever they do not achieve their ideals they go into an immediate depression, feeling they have failed completely.

Our friend Bill is an either/or thinker. Although he has several degrees and numerous certificates, experience in the military, as well as impressive artistic talent, Bill feels like an utter failure because he hasn't been able to find and hold onto a job he wants. He either succeeds totally in his occupational pursuits or he fails totally. There is no in between, no spectrum. As such, Bill serves himself a good portion of depression and self-hate.

If you feel negatively about yourself, you may very well be caught in the either/or web. Because you are not everything you want to be, you feel you are nothing. Because you are not the best spouse in the world, you feel you are the worst. Because you are not the best-looking person you ever saw, you feel you are hideous. These thoughts depress. They are neither rational nor right.

The Bible has a great deal to say about gifts, ranging from skills to personality traits. However, among its instructions is one that emphasizes that we are not to compare ourselves with others. We are unique—individuals. As such, we are to look at who we are and at what God gave us. Comparing ourselves with others can lead to arrogance on one hand; or in the case of people with depressed self-images, to a feeling of inferiority and resentment.

Paul gives good psychological advice when he says, "Be honest in your estimate of yourselves..." (Romans 12:3). Indeed, because life is usually in the middle ranges, we need to stay away from either/or polarization.

Minimaxing. [12] People who either/or their way through life, usually "minimax" as well. Minimaxing is shorthand for minimizing the positive and maximizing the negative.

Catherine is a classic minimaxer. A skilled surgical nurse, she can assist so ably in surgery that the attending physician often will compliment her. He will comment on how smoothly the surgery went, due to her conscientious preparedness in seeing that all the necessary instruments and technical apparatus are ready. However, as the physician tells her how well she performed, she reminds herself of the one surgical implement she was a tad slow to hand him. Gone, through minimaxing, is all recollection of how much responsibility she assumed and how nearly flawlessly she handled all the complicated aspects of her role. All that is present in minimaxing is that which is not perfect.

People with depressed self-images have great difficulty in thinking of anything positive about themselves, their character, or their skills. They live in a world of negative tapes which maximize with stereophonic intensity their weaknesses. As with either/or thinking, minimaxing assures that you will be depressed and self-rejecting.

Also, as with either/or thinking, minimaxing is irrational. It will not stand up to honest self-examination. We all have a variety of good and bad points in balance. Both need acknowledgment. Those positive areas need reinforcement and encouragement. The negative ones need to be worked on. Neither, however, constitutes who we are in our entirety.

Vacuum cleaning. [13] Vacuum cleaning is an extreme form of minimaxing. Here the person totally discounts anything positive—doesn't hear or see it. Instead, just like a vacuum cleaner, he pulls up any and everything negative. There is nothing to minimize since there is no awareness of anything good. People like this spend their entire mental lives finding things they can use to tell themselves what crummy people they are.

There is also a streak of paranoia in such people. At

work, they are convinced that every memo is aimed at correcting their careless behavior. Every general admonition by their employer is focused on them. Christians who vacuum clean pull up every verse in the Bible which speaks of sin and imperfection, never noticing or registering any of the assurances of God's love and grace. They feel every warning is aimed at them, every sin typifies their life; but they can find no comfort in accepting deep down that God loves them and that his only Son died to redeem them. Scripture, like everything else in life, must be viewed in balance. Vacuum cleaners have no balance at all.

Vacuum cleaning is irrational in the extreme, but very difficult to break. People who vacuum clean probably have been doing it for a long time. They live with a great deal of guilt and so spend most of their time finding things they can feel threatened or guilty about.

Sometimes simply knowing that you vacuum clean excessively can alert you to be on guard against it. Using that alertness, keep a notebook for a week, writing briefly every vacuum cleaning thought you experience. Then, at the end of the week, review your notes. There will be lots of them. However, upon review, certain vacuum cleaning thought patterns—extreme fear, guilt, or self-putdowns—will emerge. Observe these patterns, and talk back to them rationally. Simply look at them and respond to them realistically—preferably in writing, because it has a greater impact. This can break the vacuum cleaning habit. If that is difficult, it may help to open your problem up to a clergyman or therapist. A professional person's objective view can enable you to see your life more rationally.

Shoulding. [14] Shoulding is seeing all of life in terms of moral obligations—usually obligations which you feel you have not met adequately. Theresa was so deeply embedded in the "shoulds" that almost every thought contained the word "should." She was absolutely driven by real and imagined obligations. So much so that living itself became self-defeating because it amounted to little more than piling up shoulds with which she could punish herself.

I began by having Theresa keep a "should" journal. I had her write down every should for a week so she could see how enmeshed in this thinking she was. (Often "should-ers" are so driven that the shoulds become second nature mentally, and so they remain unaware of how deep a rut they are in.) After some time of looking at the frequency and intensity of her shoulds, realizing how they were hurt-ing her, Theresa was able to be moved toward talking back rationally to her shoulds. This is a process of separating reasonable from unreasonable obligations, and looking more rationally at her past performances so that she didn't always feel that she *should* have done better.

Christians who live in the "shoulds" often become legal-istic. They emphasize the law of good works at the expense of the grace of God's acceptance and forgiveness. Indeed, there are commandments for us to obey, but the reason Christ came into the world was because we are unable to live up to those laws perfectly. Accepting this relieves us of the oppression of the shoulds. Our response is not to be one of shoulding, but one of gratitude which propels us to want to honor God for his goodness and mercy. We are to be faithful and grateful, not perfect and legalistic.

Glandular Truth. [15] Glandular truth confuses feelings—glandular or physiological responses to thoughts—with truth. It is the notion that, "I feel; therefore I am"; that I am the sum total of my feelings. Hence, if I feel bad about my-self, I must be bad. If I feel guilty, I must have done some-thing wrong.

Although important, feelings are but one aspect of who we are. Moreover, feelings are not facts. They are subjec-tive, biased, intensely personal perceptions of life and real-ity. For the person with low self-esteem, the feelings become distorted. They are most definitely not to be trusted. The best way to handle the glandular truth problem is to realize you have it. Trace your feelings back to your thoughts (as we discussed earlier) and hold them up to the light of rationality, filtering out the distortions. The more rational you are, the more realistically you will see yourself. And the more realistic you are in your self-assessment, the more accepting you will be of who you are. As you feel better about your present self, you will exercise your potential to grow toward your ideal self.

The ideal self is important. In fact, it has been said that your self-esteem is measured by the size of the gap between your ideal and perceived self. For the Christian, Christ represents the ideal self. The goal is not secular self-actualization, but the mind of Christ. But here again, we have to stay out of the trap of self-punishment. We will never attain this level of perfection. Even Paul, the greatest of all Christ's apostles, said he had not reached it. So, that ideal self stands not as a whip we can use to flagellate ourselves every time we fall short of it, but rather a model of what we want to be. In stages, we can become more like Christ; and as we do, we can thank God for his help in our development.

When you fail, self-punishment is not going to help you. What will is the reminder that God accepts you and loves you as you are; and using that, you can accept yourself and move forward.

A great help in the process of improving self-esteem is the small group movement. Try getting into a therapy group of some sort.[16] Entrance into such a group does not imply psychological dysfunction. These groups are made up of people who can accept us fully and give us support in knowing and accepting ourselves.

More and more churches today have directors of counseling. Asking such a person about small group therapy is a good place to start. Once in a group, you will discover how common your problems of self-acceptance are. The compassion you will receive from others will help you accept and like yourself better. Knowing your problems are common and others enjoy being with you will greatly decrease the inner loneliness you have felt.

Intrapsychic Loneliness is no respecter of persons. However, getting to know and accept yourself is an equal opportunity enterprise. Take advantage of it. You would be amazed at what a fascinating person you are getting involved with.

CHAPTER 5

[1]Paul Tournier, *Escape from Loneliness,* translated by John S. Gilmour (Philadelphia: Westminster Press, 1977), pp. 35, 36.

[2]*Ibid.*

[3]*Ibid.,* p. 35.

[4]*Ibid.*

[5]Patricia Niles Middlebrook, *Social Psychology and Modern Life* (New York: Alfred A. Knopf, 1980), p. 53; Julian B. Rotter, "Generalized Expectancies for Internal Versus External Control of Reinforcement," *Psychological Monographs,* 80, 1, 1966.

[6]Lecture given by Dr. Wayne W. Dyer at North Park College, Chicago, Illinois, April 1982.

[7]Erik H. Erikson, "Youth and the Life Cycle," in Don E. Hamachek, *Human Dynamics in Psychology and Education* (Boston: Allyan and Bacon, 1968), p. 301.

[8]Eugene O'Neill in Middlebrook, p. 73.

[9]*New American Standard Bible.*

[10]These thought distortions are derived from *Feeling Good,* by David D. Burns (New York, Signet, 1980), pp. 28–47. This is an excellent book for overcoming depression often brought on by loneliness.

[11]Adapted from "all or nothing thinking," in Burns, p. 40.

[12]Adapted from "magnification or minimization," in Burns, p. 40.

[13]Adapted from "mental filter," in Burns, p. 40.

[14]Adapted from "should statements," in Burns, p. 40.

[15]Adapted from "emotional reasoning," in Burns, p. 40.

[16]Cecil Osborne discusses this at length in his excellent book, *The Art of Understanding Yourself* (Grand Rapids, Mich.: Zondervan, 1967).

6

SPIRITUAL
LONELINESS

Lloyd Ahlem tells the story of his involvement in a prestigious research organization focusing on an issue in public education.[1] The chairman of the organization, who was president of a corporation for psychological research, in addition to directing a successful school for emotionally disturbed children, clearly stood out for his brilliance and ability to get the most out of others. His approach was refreshing and motivating, helping the group members to keep in mind the significance of the research as they waded through mountains of paper.

One morning, the chairman was unexpectedly absent from the group meeting. The reason? He had blown his brains out with a .38 revolver the night before.

Although no one will ever know exactly why the chairman killed himself, one thing is clear. From a human standpoint, this man had it all. However, it was not enough to sustain life. After having climbed to the top of the mountain, he had no satisfactory answer to the "Is That All There Is?" question.

THE HAPPINESS AND MEANING QUEST
We live in a world in which people are looking for meaning and happiness. They thirst for a feeling of emotional well-

131

being: overall inner adequacy and peace. The chairman did not succeed in this quest. He was spiritually lonely.

People deal with happiness in three general ways.[2] One uses the concept of *comparison*. If only I were bigger, slimmer, stronger, more intelligent, or richer. Happiness is always relative and always a bit beyond where you are presently. The chase is on and never ending. The comparison criterion is an almost certain formula for unhappiness because there will always be someone better off than you.

Mary, thirty-two, was a bitter young woman. Although she was pretty, intelligent, and highly talented, she made certain she would never be happy. Mary's problem was that to be happy, she had to be beautiful; and her mother, a strikingly beautiful woman, was in Mary's estimation more beautiful than she would ever be. Mary made herself miserable through either/or thinking. Either she was as beautiful as her mother—and hence happy—or she was ugly and depressed.

Another common method employs the concept of *circumstance*. If only I had a little more money, or lived in a more pleasant climate, or could get "the breaks" and land the job I always wanted. Here you want to be transported from a present unhappy or at least less than fulfilling situation to another, more positive one. That move is supposed to spell happiness.

This concept is also psychological fool's gold. You will never be in an earthly circumstance which could not be improved. Ellen, a very accomplished and bright woman in her thirties, never seemed happy. Perfectionism drove her to see every circumstance in her life as less than fully satisfying. A teacher, she did not feel she was as effective as she should be with her students; a seamstress, she did not feel her work was of quality; a homemaker, she was not satisfied with the appearance of her home. Ellen was a slave to the tyranny of happiness through circumstance—the it-could-be-better syndrome.

There is also the concept of *change*. I have a friend named

John. He is in his thirties and has held more jobs than I can count. He is a walking employment directory. The pattern has always been the same. He would take a job, tell me all the advantages of it, and how well he liked it. After six months he would call and I would ask him, "How's the job going?"

"I need a change," he would answer restlessly. And sure enough, within weeks he would make a change, and then the cycle would start all over again. It was so regular that he actually found himself going full circle in one case—working the very same job he had left three years before.

People who search for happiness, bent on the change method, are always making alterations in their life. They may change marriage partners, jobs, apartments, or hobbies. There is a feeling of going nowhere—stagnating—and so making changes is the answer. However, as with the other two concepts, there is no end point. Although they are moving, too often—like John—it is in a circle, not forward.

Beyond these ways of seeking happiness, people are tempted to look for happiness in achievement.[3] For many who have never achieved much, this seems to be the nirvana. If only I could open a successful business; if only I could be a renowned artist; if only I could get that job, then I would be happy are all common thoughts.

There are two problems with looking for happiness and meaning in achievement. One is that, like circumstance and change, there is rarely any end to the quest. No sooner do you graduate from high school, and it's college. Upon college graduation, it's graduate school, and on and on. Almost regardless of the achievement, once it is experienced and celebrated, you'll find yourself thinking of doing something a bit more challenging. One's reach for achievement almost invariably exceeds one's grasp.

The second problem is often even worse. It was the chairman's problem. You might attain your ultimate goal only to discover it is far less satisfying than you thought it would be.

I have a friend who is a big league baseball star. He explained that from the cradle his father steered him toward a career in baseball, with the crowning goal being a huge, multi-year contract. After coming through the lower ranks, living the bologna-and-cheese life of the minor leagues, and struggling through the early major league years, he finally established himself. He was a star and his ball club wanted to sign him to a long-term contract. This was the zenith—what he had dedicated his life to. The negotiating completed, the day finally came and he marched triumphantly into the team office and signed a six-year pact worth nearly four million dollars. His financial future was set in cement.

But he wasn't happy.

"When I drove home from the team office," he said slowly, "I began to cry."

For my big league friend, the experience was one of the most painful of his entire life. He had discovered that the thing he had invested life in was not satisfying at all. He had gotten what he had sought to achieve and it was plastic rather than gold. He felt ripped off, depressed. Anything but fulfilled.

His story is not unusual. I don't know of a single accomplished person who attributes his happiness and meaning to those accomplishments. In fact, the "Is That All There Is?" feeling is so widespread, you may have heard the proverb of warning: Beware of what you want most in life; you may get it.

Possessions and wealth are the goals of millions. For them, a new house, a new car, a new stereo, new furniture, or some other expensive item holds the key to meaning and fulfillment. Like achievement, possessions tend to bring short-term gratification, piling up and going unappreciated as our attention shifts to pulling in the next prize. Adults become merely grown-up versions of children who pine away for a certain birthday present, convinced that once they receive it, they will be truly happy. The birthday comes, the present is unwrapped and enthused over for several days—only to bring a wish for an even more ultimate Christmas or birthday gift. The problem with regarding possessions as the key to happiness is seen in the apocryphal story of the rich man who was asked, "How much money would it take to make you happy?"

"Just a little more," he replied.

If wealth, achievement, and material possessions could bring happiness and inner peace, people like Elvis Presley, Freddie Prinze, and John Belushi would not have destroyed themselves. They each got what they really thought they wanted out of life and were left with an empty plate for the starving inner person.

More educated people often search for meaning and happiness in intellectuality, dealing with life at a very deep and abstract level. They feel that the more they know, the better decisions they will make, and the more enriched their lives will be. Somehow in the quest for learning and understanding, they believe truth will be uncovered and the mysteries of life will become clear.

Though intellectual pursuits can be very stimulating, like achievements, they have a temporary effect at best. Perhaps the most brilliant man I ever studied under in my graduate experience was a philosopher who found no meaning in life. Life to him was "a mass of absurdities." He hadn't stopped looking or reading, and I am sure he is still learning; but at last notice, his studies had not yielded truth and meaning.

There is also the path of withdrawal. The 60s were filled with young people who saw their parents choking on wealth and decadence, only to find themselves miserable and directionless. So, these youths decided to withdraw—drop out. The "hippie" life style—replete with drugs, free love, and communal togetherness—seemed the panacea.

Now these people are in their thirties. Many are still here but their communes and radical life styles have been abandoned. They have traded in their beads for a tie, and their leather coats for a suit, as they have moved into the establishment they once condemned their parents for being a part of. In fact, many of them are bitter that they spent so much of their early adult life in a holding pattern.

Withdrawal is still big today. The drug culture is filled with people dropping out. Young people adrift in an autistic world of marijuana, cocaine, and other pharmaceuticals, accompanied by blaring stereos and a party atmosphere, represent a new generation which is withdrawing. They are human testimonies that the materialistic lives of their parents do not appeal. Tragically, however, I have yet to meet a single person who has gone the withdrawal route and does not regret it.

Sometimes the quest for meaning and inner peace takes a humanitarian turn. We look for meaning in good deeds—acts of charity and mercy. Though more fulfilling than the previous paths, humanitarianism for its own sake often gives way to emotional burnout. You give and give and give, but the problems don't go away. There are still children who can't read, people without jobs, and families trapped in poverty. You are left with exhaustion and the gnawing, guilt-ridden question, "Did I do enough?" For every one you help, there are ten more people out there waiting.

Dr. William Leslie, renowned pastor of Chicago's LaSalle Street Church, tells of the burnout experienced when humanitarianism is viewed as the way of salvation: "I remember that in the 60s the only ministries in this community, other than ours, were carried on by very liberal churches—churches who thought the key to salvation and meaning was social action. Now they are all gone. They burned out. Realizing they were never going to solve all the problems, and that the human standards of success they believed in would not be attained, they became depressed and gave up."[4]

A famous former big leaguer being feted in his hometown also found that neither achievement nor humanitarianism could bring inner adequacy and spiritual peace. He had distinguished himself as an all-time great with over

3,000 base hits and had won major humanitarian awards for his sacrificial involvement in charitable causes. After having his accomplishments on the field and in community service recited, he rose amid a thunderous ovation to speak. He looked out into the audience and said simply, "There must be more to life than this," and then sat down to a stunned silence.

All this is not to demean humanitarianism. As Christians, we are enjoined to love our neighbor as ourselves. Compassion for others which translates into service is absolutely necessary. However, for humanitarianism to be truly satisfying and enduring, it must spring from a deeper spiritually fulfilling motivation. Humanitarian deeds, performed while one is suffering from Spiritual Loneliness, are rarely fulfilling.

In short, you will never find happiness, peace, fulfillment, emotional well-being, or what I call an overall sense of inner adequacy by chasing it. It is not something you can capture or attain. In fact, one of the universal laws of human behavior is that the more you chase this sense of inner adequacy, the further away it seems to be; after you reach each milestone, you are still no closer.

HUMAN STANDARDS

In fact, if a sense of inner adequacy could be met by reaching some human standard, you would have to ask some serious questions. Human standards are by nature unfair. Over half the world has less than sufficient means for healthy living. Literally millions go to bed each night hungry, while countless others die of starvation.

Even in America, there is nothing approaching fairness in terms of opportunity to reach human standards such as achievement and wealth. People vary according to what family they are born into, what color their skin is, what schools they attended, and what inheritance they will receive. The children of the rich tend to become rich; the middle class, middle class; the poor, poorer. The great fact of American life is that you are what you are largely because you were born that way, rather than because you achieved it in an atmosphere of fair competition.

Human standards also change. Clothing styles, car sizes, corporate systems, and standards for physical appearance are constantly shifting. Having had it made in the 50s may mean nothing today, unless you have adjusted to every changing tide. A high school degree in the 30s made you a well educated person. Today graduate training is a minimum standard. Human standards will not yield a sense of inner peace and adequacy. They never have. The best they have to offer is brief and transitory happiness—the happiness of temporary celebration and satisfaction over some attainment.

Chasing these human standards results ultimately in the feeling of emptiness. Even worse, there is often a feeling of guilt for being alive while failing to find real meaning in life—having no ultimate reason to justify your existence. This business of justifying our existence is important. I remember an incident regarding an interview with a famous gossip columnist. She was cruising right along, fielding questions from an appreciative audience when someone asked, "How do you, as a gossip columnist, justify your existence?"

The arrogance melted and the woman became highly defensive, suggesting that although she had scaled great human heights, she had no real answer to that more ultimate question.

CHRISTIANITY

One of the strongest arguments for the truth of Christianity is that it gives people a reason for living. According to the New Testament, you are an object of supreme love, an individual whose value and significance lie in being created by Almighty God for the purpose of honoring and serving him.

If you look in the New Testament, you will see that God views the Christian—one who commits his life to his Son, Jesus, as Savior and center of his life—as adequate.[5]

First, to God you are very expensive. You were bought with a price. The cost was the blood of his own Son, Jesus Christ, necessary to forgive your wrongs and make you acceptable to a perfect God. This latter point is absolutely critical and much more than an abstract foray into theology. It is that acceptance of you as perfect in God's eyes which makes you totally adequate. In fact, the writer of Hebrews says that for the Christian, Christ is his brother.

The Christian is no longer chained to the guilt of the past —the feelings of uselessness and inadequacy. He is liberated from that, enabling him to live out his life in gratitude for God's bringing him into the inner circle of the divine Family.

Spiritual Loneliness is dispelled by this newfound closer-than-a-brother relationship with the Son of God, Jesus Christ, one that is strengthened by the freedom from guilt and alienation you experience even though you are not and never will be perfect.

The miracle in all this is that experiencing it does not involve human performance or human standards in any way. You get it by receiving—choosing—accepting God's love, a love which in no way compares with any other love we have experienced.

LOVE

According to the ancient Greeks, there are three kinds of love. One is erotic love. This refers to sexual love, or passion. It can be a beautiful form of love, one of great excitement and intimacy, but it is also easily exploited. Our society is filled with exploitation of this kind of love. We hear of it everywhere—from TV to popular music about "making love." In most cases, no love is made at all. Sex is simply performed.

One young girl couldn't understand God's love. Upon hearing of it she said it left her cold. "As far as I am concerned," she said, "it means God wants to have sex with me. I have had enough of that kind of love."

A second form of love is filial or brotherly love. This kind of love exists within loving families and among intimate yet platonic friends. It is more stable, though less exciting, than erotic love. Its value lies in its consistency and openness.

Once we have received Christ into our lives, we are able to dispel a good deal of Loneliness Out as well as Spiritual Loneliness, by claiming the filial love we have with Christ and his Father. However, when we think of God's love, we are usually referring to a love much greater than this.

That love is *agape* love—love without condition or strings. It is free for the taking. Its free nature is extremely difficult to comprehend. We are so used to paying for everything in this "no free lunches" culture, the notion of agape love can leave us skeptical. The concept of earning approval is so deeply embedded that often we have difficulty accepting favors from even the closest of friends because we feel duty-bound to return them at some future point. In fact, I am certain you know of several people who will do what appears to be a freely given favor, only to remember it and hold it over your head for repayment at a desired moment.

But again, agape love is free. It can't be bought, earned, or achieved. It is offered. As such, it is a great equalizer. Age, sex, race, and income level are irrelevant when it comes to agape love. All the human barriers we erect are inapplicable. We all have equal claim to it.

Moreover, it is pure.[6] There are no petty jealousies or hangups in agape love. You don't have to adjust to the idiosyncracies of a friend or a family member to keep on receiving it. God and his love are bigger than that.

It is also personal.[7] You are not brought into God's inner family through some impersonal credit card system. There has never been, is not, nor ever will be anyone exactly like you among all the billions of creatures on the earth. It is the same Creator, the one who fashioned you in that uniqueness, who is offering you agape love. Moreover, it is given in the form of a person—Jesus Christ—not a set of laws and qualifications. This is what "a personal relationship with Jesus Christ" means. It is intensely personal, individual, and unique. Although you are saved from the ruin of your sin by the same death and resurrection as everyone else, your personal relationship with God is just that—personal. It is similar but never identical to anyone else's. This is the beauty of agape love. It is what takes the impersonality—the loneliness—out of your spirit.

The more you ponder the depth of God's love, love which is extended to you in this life and beyond, the more amazing it becomes. It begins defying all human imagination and brings with it such a groundswell of spiritual joy that you feel overcome.

Nevertheless, some people have particular difficulty accepting, much less experiencing, agape love. Those who have had troubled childhoods, experienced extreme forms of interpersonal rejection, or who have particularly poor self-concepts, find the notion of agape love almost beyond comprehension. This, however, makes agape love no less a fact.

Tony, fifty, had been all but abandoned as a child. He had been so traumatized by family conflict, that he became psychosomatically ill and was hospitalized at eight years old. While in the hospital, he was treated coldly and rebelled out of fear. As a result of a defiant comment, an insensitive physician ordered him placed in the adult psychiatric ward among dangerously insane people. Eight-year-old Tony, after this series of betrayals, pleaded desperately with God to get him out of there. Almost as he was praying, a distant family relative was demanding that his parents get him out of that institution and bring him home with them.

Today, Tony does believe in God, but due to a lifetime filled with human rejection, finds it very difficult to trust the love of anyone. The slightest sign of betrayal or artificiality sets him off. He becomes extremely suspicious and rejecting in return. Although agape love is incredibly liberating, it is very hard to accept.

Parents, however well meaning, can often stand in the way. One young woman, upon hearing that God was her Father, said that such a concept was less than zero for her. Her father had been such a negative, cruel force in her life, that if God was anything like him, she wanted nothing to do with God.

Some of the same thought distortions we discussed in the previous chapter block the experience of agape love, bringing about Spiritual Loneliness. When vacuum cleaners read Scripture, all the warnings and admonitions appear to them in bold print, and all the love, grace, and forgiveness in fine print. The result is that you see nothing but sin in yourself. You condemn yourself as a person who does absolutely nothing of value in God's kingdom. You regard yourself as a complete spiritual failure whom no one, certainly not a perfect God, can possibly love.

Minimaxing is almost as bad. Although you can detect traces of God's grace in your life, you downplay your value as a servant of Christ, while highlighting your failure. You discount yourself as a growing, developing child of God, who is being used in ever greater ways, but rather regard yourself as a stumbling spiritual klutz.

A good exercise to deal with vacuum cleaning and minimaxing is to work at internalizing the love of God by studying the form it took in Christ's life in the Gospels. Read especially the book of John, with an eye toward Christ's love and care for others. Focusing specifically on this love will reverse the vacuum-cleaning tendency of some Christians.

There are other exercises which can also be of help. One is to study the epistles in the New Testament, underlining every passage which speaks of God's love and care. Then take those verses and read and reread them. Commit the most personally meaningful ones to memory and use them to talk back to the irrational feelings arising from vacuum cleaning and minimaxing.

Either/or thinking is also a problem. In this thinking, the moment you fall short of some perfectionist standard, you slide all the way down into the emotional pit of feeling utterly worthless. Instead of seeing yourself as going through the stages of gaining spiritual maturity, the slightest slip leaves you devastated. This becomes especially irrational when you consider that you cannot really do anything, from getting out of bed to keeping God's commandments, without his help. When you fail, instead of indulging in self-hate and punishment, you need only to reaffirm your faith in God's care and power to get back on the track.

A good way of counteracting the either/or tendency is to study the growth in spiritual maturity in the lives of Christ's disciples. As you follow their lives in the Gospels and on into the book of Acts, you will see how they grew from virtual embryos to spiritual giants. However, their growth, like yours, was a process. Either/or thinking denies the concept of process and robs you of the growth experience.

To dispel Spiritual Loneliness, you have to choose to open your life and receive agape love. Without it, there is a gnawing alienation, an emptiness in the inner person. It can be no different. As children of God, our ignoring him is a form of running away from our spiritual Parent. There is no real peace there. To say that those who do not believe are on their way to hell does not sound so radical and judgmental when you consider that hell is nothing more than total alienation, total separation from God. While alive, we have an opportunity to bridge that alienation and go back to our Maker. But to the extent that we turn our backs on agape love, we experience a good bit of hell right now.

As for the commandments of God, they are there not to frustrate us by making life difficult, or to dish up a bit of conditional love and grist for guilt. They exist to show us how to live with maximum meaning and long-term satisfaction.

God's commandments can be likened to the material contained in the owner's manual you receive when you buy a new car. If you ignore that manual and operate the car carelessly, it will not run as long or as well as if you followed the manual carefully. The use of the manual does require some self-discipline; but in the long term, it pays off. Similarly, following the commandments of God has long-term benefits, and living in defiance of them, although temporarily pleasurable, does not yield ultimate happiness and peace.

As children of God, we are ultimately dependent on him, whether or not we admit it. Tournier explains that each independent attitude and extreme form of individuality is, in the final analysis, a revolt against God.[8] We will not gain ultimate peace within ourselves or with our fellow humans unless we rediscover God's presence and centrality in our lives.

Without the inner peace and adequacy which come from agape love, it is easy to stay unintegrated people. We can indulge in self-analysis and learn to feel better about ourselves at some levels, but at the same time, we are often driven farther away from fellow human beings, because we don't feel free and secure to love and be loved completely.

We are not at peace with ourselves and so we have difficulty being at peace with others. Beyond the feelings of low self-esteem mentioned earlier, and the lack of purpose and meaning in life, we fall prey to resentment and bitterness when others do not give us our due. Moreover, it can be very difficult to forgive because we do not feel forgiven in our inner self and at peace with God.

You may, however, have made a commitment to Christ and still feel desolate inside. There is no real peace, no joy, but rather a painful, diffused sense of guilt and anxiety. If so, you are most likely muddled in one or more of the thought distortions mentioned earlier, concentrating on your imperfections and sin—sin which is removed by your acceptance of Christ—rather than focusing on the limitless agape love of God for you.

There is no better example of this inability to focus on agape love than the experience of Norman, an elderly man who has lived his entire life in devoted Christian service to others and his church. Despite all the sermons and personal affirmations of God's grace and mercy, Norman still occasionally wakes up in the middle of the night in a cold sweat over a fear of God's reprisals for sins committed and confessed years ago. Norman is not concentrating on agape love. He is not allowing himself to experience it.

Norman needs to take his cue from Paul, who regarded the love of God as more important and more powerful than anything else. He says:

> For I am convinced that nothing can ever separate us from his love. Death can't, and life can't. The angels won't, and all the powers of hell itself cannot keep God's love away. Our fears for today, our worries about tomorrow, or where we are—high above the sky, or in the deepest ocean—nothing will ever be able to separate us from the love of God demonstrated by our Lord Jesus Christ when he died for us (Romans 8:38, 39, TLB).

Ron also had problems. He was brought up in a devoutly Christian home but never felt close to God. He sowed his wild oats in adolescence and early adulthood in order to test the terrain on the other side. But that brought no real satisfaction either. In his thirties, he would plead with tears and desperation to God for some sense of peace and spiritual closeness. He was spiritually lonely in the extreme.

Ron's problem was that, despite all the preachments to

the contrary, he had been raised with a guilt-imputing conditional love. His father and mother modeled this conditional strings-attached form of love and so, as his human
examples of what God is like, he never could feel God's
presence. It was not until Ron came to see his parents more
realistically, as the imperfect couple they were rather than as
mini-Christs, that he could experience God's love with
maximum impact. He could see that God did not deal in a
hammer-over-the-head fashion, but rather as one who
wanted to liberate him from the guilt of his imperfections.
God was no longer some divine attorney general in the sky,
but rather a loving Father who forgave and cared.

Ron's case illustrates why you can sometimes get better
fellowship in the average bar than in the church. The reason
is that there is often a lack of acceptance and unconditional
love in the church. People burdened down with feelings of
guilt and spiritual discomfort tend to deal with others in a
judgmental way. They don't feel accepted by God, cannot
accept themselves, and so have great difficulty accepting
others.

The key to eradicating much Spiritual Loneliness through
a reunion with God is in separating God from all the faulty
human models we have been presented with, and then
looking at God as he is presented in Christ. In fact, if you
want to know what God is like, simply look at his Son—
Jesus Christ. A close reading of the book of John will reveal
Christ in all his love, care, and compassion. Moreover, as
mentioned earlier, a good technique you can use in helping
you experience God's love is to study the form it took in
Christ's life throughout the Gospels. Reading them, focusing exclusively on all his many expressions of love and care
for others, can be eye opening. In fact, prayer, along with
studying and memorizing key passages in the epistles, can
be highly effective.

There are also some good auto-suggestion techniques
which can be valuable in experiencing God's closeness. One
is to repeat the words, "Jesus loves me now," four times

emphasizing the name, Jesus, the first time; "loves," the second time; and so forth. Do this when you start the day in the morning and before you go to sleep at night. Saturating your mind daily with these words plants them in your subconscious so that over time they become more and more a part of your spiritual outlook. Eventually you will find these words leaping into your consciousness whenever you feel a sense of Spiritual Loneliness.

Another mental technique is to say these words while picturing yourself in the arms of Jesus. Visualizing God's love in this way adds an additional dimension to the experience. Combining these two experiences can work wonders over time.

Once you have internalized agape love, you are free of the tyranny of arbitrary, unfair, and changing human standards. You are adequate by a much greater standing than any earthly one. You are now excused from the neurosis of having to chase happiness, peace, and inner adequacy through human performance. The pressure of the never-ending grind toward meaning through human effort is removed.

The new criteria for healthy living shifts from performance and success to faithfulness. Your focus is on strengthening your faith and reliance on God's love and power rather than on a series of must-do behaviors to win God's approval. The more you come to grips with this new perspective on adequacy, the more the sense of failure fades. You assess yourself as an object of supreme love and care rather than against the backdrop of others' human expectations.

This rarely happens overnight, even in the case of the most dramatic born-again experiences. The reason is that absolutely nothing in our culture supports this way of seeing ourselves and life. The impression of having to prove yourself by your performance is everywhere. Not only is your worth in your job determined solely on performance, but you are rarely free of it even in the most accepting of family settings. If you fail to treat loved ones the way they want to be treated, you will eventually find that even they will reject you. Appearance, achievement, and others' expectations surround us as bases for acceptance.

SELF-CONCEPT

The more you see God rationally, as the all-loving person he really is, the more clearly you can see your spiritual self.

You will realize, first of all, that you are a common person.[9] In Romans 3:22, 23, Paul points out that, "God says he will accept and acquit us—declare us 'not guilty'—if we trust Jesus Christ to take away our sins. And we all can be saved in this same way, by coming to Christ, no matter who we are or what we have been like. Yes, all have sinned; all fall short of God's glorious ideal."

There is no basis here to separate people according to skin color, income, sex, or age. You share the same human condition with everyone. You are no worse in that all of humanity needs to receive God's agape love, but certainly you are no better either. Self-righteousness is mere foolishness. You are put right with God, not on your own merits or performance, something which can waver very quickly, but on accepting God's forgiveness through Christ his Son. As such, your Spiritual Loneliness is dispelled by letting God in, rather than by striving to earn his love.

You are a supremely valuable person—bought, as previously mentioned, with the highest of prices—the blood of the Son of God.[10] The concept of being bought is liberating rather than enslaving. You no longer belong solely to yourself so that you have to strive for emotional stability, proper appearance, and socially acceptable behavior on your own. You are now grafted into God's family, and as such your well-being now and forever is secure.

You are now free to become all you can be without the attendant fears of self-achieved adequacy.[11] Paul echoes this freedom in 2 Corinthians 5:13, 14 (TLB), when he says,

"Are we insane [to say such things about ourselves]? If so, it is to bring glory to God. And if we are in our right minds, it is for your benefit. Whatever we do, it is certainly not for our own profit, but because Christ's love controls us now. Since we believe that Christ died for all of us, we should also believe that we have died to the old life we used to live."

Paul isn't concerned about his sanity or insanity. He is what God wants him to be. He no longer has to concern himself with his own needs. In verse 15, he points out the freeing effect of Christ's death, claiming that, "He died for all so that all who live—having received eternal life from him—might live no longer for themselves, to please themselves, but to spend their lives pleasing Christ who died and rose again for them."

Human standards are no longer the criteria. They need not plague us; we have a larger vision. "So stop evaluating Christians by what the world thinks about them or by what they seem to be like on the outside. Once I mistakenly thought of Christ that way, merely as a human being like myself. How differently I feel now! When someone becomes a Christian he becomes a brand new person inside. He is not the same anymore. A new life has begun!" (2 Corinthians 5:16, 17).

And all of this breaks through the Spiritual Loneliness because, "All these new things are from God, who brought us back to himself through what Christ Jesus did. And God has given us the privilege of urging everyone to come into his favor and be reconciled to him. For God was in Christ, restoring the world to himself, no longer counting men's sins against them but blotting them out. This is the wonderful message he has given us to tell others" (2 Corinthians 5:18, 19).

As a result of this new relationship with Christ, you are viewed by God as a flawless person. There is no longer any basis for guilt. The loneliness and estrangement that sin brings are broken because " . . . there is now no condemnation awaiting those who belong to Christ Jesus" (Romans 8:1). Consequently, the corrosive effect of constant guilt, unworthiness, and inadequacy is irrational. By Christ's work and our acceptance of his love, we are viewed by God as no different, not one bit more guilty than Christ is.

Paul asks rhetorically, "Who dares accuse us whom God has chosen for his own? Will God? No! He is the one who has forgiven us and given us right standing with himself" (Romans 8:33). The next time someone lays a guilt trip on you, you can tell him that, by the grace of God, you are no longer a guilty person. You are controlled by your desire to be more like Christ rather than free from guilt and divine punishment.

Spiritual Loneliness is really broken by your awareness that you are a known person.[12] No matter how hidden, blind, and locked your human Johari Window, you are transparent to God. In Romans 8:27, we are reminded that God knows all human hearts; and, "Yes, he knows the secrets of every heart" (Psalm 44:21). That X-ray knowledge is no basis for fear when we remember we are innocent in God's eyes. Rather, it gives us certain knowledge that as others disappoint us, let us down, and fail to understand us, God is different. We are not lonely in our spiritual being because he is inside us, knowing and caring about every pain we experience.

If you are ever on the island of Spiritual Loneliness, doubting whether God cares about your well-being, all you have to do is read the opening and closing sections of the New Testament epistles. They repeatedly refer to grace and peace for believers. If you are familiar with Scripture, you have probably read these words—grace and peace—hundreds of times, and perhaps they have had no impact on you at all. If the Bible is new to you, they may seem strange and archaic. In any case, let's take a closer look at these words.

In Greek, grace refers to joy, pleasure, and beauty.[13]

Through Christ, grace takes on the meaning of making the beauty of life brighter and more lovely because we are free from the oppression of having to be good. We are now truly children of God.

In addition, grace suggests total, unmerited generosity; a gift of beauty, charm, and sweetness which is completely unearned. It is the divine equivalent of having a warm, caring, and giving person enter your life to bring you a sweetness, beauty, and charm you have not known.

Peace denotes a harmonious weaving together.[14] Here the believer, without the burdens of guilt and fear, is joined with God. He is blended together in intimacy with other Christians; and the various parts of his personality are integrated into a unified, organized whole. Peace conveys the idea of the highest level of well-being, optimal functioning. It is the opposite of loneliness, alienation, estrangement, and anxiety.

A good exercise is to note these two gifts of God, grace and peace. Study them carefully in terms of their full meanings just discussed. Then, in writing, note how each of these can and does apply to your life. Writing is much better than simply reflecting about them because it has a much greater impact. Review your life in terms of how you have received grace and peace in the past and where you need to claim them now. At all times, bear in mind that grace and peace can be claimed at any time. They are present—available now; God guarantees that through his promises.

Once you have written how you relate to grace and peace, use what you have written in your periods of solitude. Think through grace and peace, rehearse them, and add to your writing until the reality of these gifts seeps into the depths of your conscious and subconscious mind. Keep in mind that these are promises that the most famous of all saints, among them the Apostle Paul, embraced in the grimmest of circumstances—while experiencing imprisonment, persecution, and the loneliness which arises from the abandonment and rejection of friends. They gave and still give a spiritual power which has been coveted by people for centuries.

Paul, for example, found an end to Spiritual Loneliness by claiming these promises. It was enough to sustain him when he faced every other type of loneliness: The Loneliness In from having those he wanted to communicate with not understand him; the Loneliness Out resulting from being abandoned by others; his Intrapsychic Loneliness which arose in part from being put through all types of earthly changes; and the general loneliness of being in prison and exile. Paul knew the power of these promises, the power which enabled him, by living close to God, to live above his circumstances.

They can do the same for you.

CHAPTER 6

[1] Lloyd H. Ahlem, *Do I Have to Be Me?* (Ventura, Cal.: Regal Books, 1973), pp. 55, 56.

[2] Sermon by David Burnham given at LaSalle Street Church, Chicago, Illinois, January 20, 1980.

[3] Lecture given by Lloyd H. Ahlem at the Broken Wall, Chicago, Illinois, March 23, 1971. In his presentation, Dr. Ahlem discussed achievement and a variety of other ways in which people search for happiness, many of which are reviewed in the subsequent pages.

[4] Private conversation with Dr. Leslie; also reviewed in *The Reluctant Defender*, by David Claerbaut (Wheaton, Ill.: Tyndale House Publishers, 1978), p. 222.

[5] Ahlem, March 23, 1971.

[6] Paul Tournier, *Escape from Loneliness*, translated by John S. Gilmour (Philadelphia: Westminster Press, 1977), p. 114.

[7] Tournier discusses several characteristics of love on pp. 113–116.

[8] *Ibid.*, p. 63.

[9] Chapel presentation by Lloyd H. Ahlem while he was President of North Park College, Chicago, Illinois.

[10] *Ibid.*

[11] Ahlem, March 23, 1971.

[12] Ahlem, chapel presentation.

[13] The material on grace is developed in William Barclay, *The Letters to the Philippians, Colossians, and Thessalonians* (Philadelphia: Westminster Press, 1975), p. 12; William Barclay, *The Letters to Timothy, Titus, and Philemon* (Philadelphia: Westminster Press, 1975), pp. 23, 24.

[14] *Ibid.*

SITUATIONAL
LONELINESS

Situational Loneliness is a temporary state due to circumstances often beyond our control. Though less painful and intense than the previously discussed types of loneliness, it is the most common. In fact, while you may not suffer from any of the other kinds, you will have a hard time avoiding Situational Loneliness. So it must be faced.

If you never experience Situational Loneliness it may be a bad sign. You may very well be programming yourself so heavily that you never have to be alone. Believe me, if you never experience Situational Loneliness, you are probably running from it. Situational Loneliness is a normal, natural part of being alive.

In fact, overly active people are often less devoted to the activities they are "committed" to, than they are to avoiding any form of loneliness. Janet, forty-three, is among the most likable people I have ever met. Absolutely everyone appreciates her. Single and living in a condominium, Janet is always on the go. During the week, she works in a downtown office in a major city, dealing with people all day on the phone. On weekends, she works the desk for a suburban motel. These two jobs, along with outings with friends and involvement in her church, give Janet a full life.

Though Janet enjoys these activities, her principal reason for scheduling herself so heavily is that she is terrified at the prospect of being alone. All but abandoned by her father as a child, Janet has deep-seated insecurity and has dealt with it by developing some very effective social skills. Being liked is so important to her that she finds almost any argument disturbing; she will apologize even if she feels she was right. At the conscious level, she fears hurting others' feelings. Unconsciously, however, she is afraid of rejection. Being alone for Janet means being lonely. And being lonely brings on childhood sensations of rejection and abandonment.

DISGUISES

Moreover, how you handle Situational Loneliness is a good measure of how you are able to deal with the more serious forms of loneliness. In fact, it is easy to mistake Situational Loneliness for other, more profound types.

Harriet, fifty-eight, who lived with her husband and granddaughter, appeared to be rather strong, vibrant, and well-adjusted woman. However, once she began telling me about the possibility of her granddaughter leaving to live with her out-of-state daughter, Harriet started crying.

Probing further, it became obvious that Harriet was not simply fearing the Situational Loneliness resulting from not seeing her granddaughter. That loneliness was disguising a deeper problem of Loneliness In. Her husband, a successful businessman, cared little about Harriet and had had several affairs. They hadn't slept together for years.

As a result, Harriet had built her social world around her granddaughter to buttress her psyche against the torment of Loneliness In. Now she was in peril of being deprived of her only defense. Her loneliness, therefore, was not temporary, and dealing with the loss of her grand-daughter would prove no ultimate solution. For Harriet, it was time to confront her marriage and determine what her options were.

Jim and Marie had never really had a honeymoon. So, after their children were several years old, Jim, longing to be alone with Marie without the distractions of the children, suggested that they take a trip—just the two of them—to Canada, on the money he had saved.

Marie welcomed the idea and soon they left for Canada. They had hardly crossed the border before Marie became severely depressed. She spent the entire "honeymoon" in her hotel room, disinterested in the sights and activities available for tourists. Not long after their return, Marie had the first of several affairs which started a long journey toward the destruction of their marriage.

Although no one could say that Marie, without her children and friends was *not* experiencing Situational Loneliness in Canada, it is obvious that she had been experiencing a good deal of Loneliness In a lot longer. Once in Canada with Jim, her substitutes for marital fulfillment were gone and the emptiness she had been denying to herself and to Jim came crashing through in the form of a depression.

If you asked Tara, an attractive, exuberant twenty-five-year-old woman, she would tell you she experiences Situational Loneliness. In reality, Tara suffers from Loneliness Out. Because she usually has a man in her life, her bouts with loneliness are only periodic, occurring after fights or other mini-breakups. However, the moment Tara loses a relationship, she goes into a panic. She surrounds herself with friends, canvasses the singles bars looking for company, and uses the telephone as a life-support system. In short, Tara is a "people junkie," longing for an intimacy she has never experienced. Thus far, she has managed, through the clever use of her attractiveness and other forms of manipulation, never to be without a relationship for long, making it appear that her loneliness is merely situational. However, until she deals with her Loneliness Out terror, she will find little peace.

Situational Loneliness can also camouflage Intrapsychic Loneliness. John, the young man who couldn't complete a simple assignment of being alone for a brief period each week, thought he suffered from Situational Loneliness. However, people protected him from his intensely negative self-image and the immobilizing effect of having to be his own company. Until John musters the courage to confront his deep-seated identity problems, he will continue to fool himself by thinking his loneliness is only occasional and due to circumstance.

Richard, the entertainer who was so severely depressed he could hardly take a shower, also thought his loneliness was situational, describing it as more acute sometimes than other times. However, Richard was not only intrapsychically lonely (as we discussed in chapter 5), but spiritually lonely as well. In his fifties, and feeling too old to be sexually attractive to the women he longed to get involved with, his outlook on life was suffused with a sense of meaninglessness and purposelessness. Death, although hardly dreaded in view of how depressing life seemed, was all he could see on the horizon; and it held no promise of peace or fulfillment either since he considered himself an agnostic. Again, the apparent Situational Loneliness had much deeper roots.

STIMULATION

Situational Loneliness is often accompanied by a sudden drop in social stimulation. We live our lives accustomed to a certain amount of activity. When that activity level—stimulation—drops sharply for a significant period of time (such as days and weeks), a feeling of loneliness often sets in.

This is why weekends are particularly difficult for single

adults who have people-oriented jobs. They work all week in an office buzzing with social stimulation, then as Friday night closes in, they face a weekend devoid of human contact. This also explains why singles often experience intense depression when they lose their jobs. For them, job loss is not simply a loss of income. It is loss of contact with the human world.

The more socially active we are in our daily routines, the more acutely we will experience any loss of stimulation. We become so accustomed to having others around, responding to us, that the absence of company leaves us with a sense of lifelessness. Without realizing it, our sense of significance has become so deeply anchored in relations with others, that having no one around can bring on a sense of worthlessness.

The high voltage nature of life makes loneliness even more difficult. We touched on this in the first chapter. Those of us who are extremely busy are almost never alone —or at least unoccupied. This can produce tremendous amounts of Intrapsychic and Spiritual Loneliness of which we are unaware, until the curve on our stimulation graph slopes and a sense of panic sets in.

Ben, a much-in-demand minister in the East, is an "activityaholic." He schedules breakfast meetings at 7:00 A.M., races through his day, and manages to be gone almost every evening. As he is immensely popular and outgoing, people tend to see Ben as the ideal person. However, having avoided any reduced speed zones and the Situational Loneliness which can accompany them, Ben has developed an intense amount of Intrapsychic Loneliness. It shows in his discomfort with pastoral counseling situations and one-to-one pastoring. Hearing others' emotional and personal hurts triggers the pain of his own confusion and undealt with inner conflicts. Moreover, Ben admits he has to force himself to schedule times of solitude to curtail the tendency to develop Situational Loneliness.

If you live a high-speed life like Ben's, it is extremely important to build into it periods of solitude and relaxation. You need to balance out your life's rhythms so that you have periods of high, medium, and low stimulation. The more you schedule these changes of pace into your life pattern, the more prepared you will be if and when the stimulation needle drops to zero. Moreover, you will learn to enjoy rather than dread vacations. Whereas they used to trigger depressions due to a sense of lost significance, you will come to look forward to them. You will have learned to enjoy being, as well as doing. Passivity as well as activity.

CHANGES IN LIFE STYLE

Sooner or later, the stimulation curve will slope and Situational Loneliness will emerge. Often a downturn occurs with a change in life style. For many women, stimulation drops when children reach school age. Suddenly there is no one sending you constant messages of being needed and depended upon. In addition, if your marriage is not idyllic, you may, like Harriet, find yourself feeling lonely, frightened, and depressed.

This experience is intensified when the children are older and "leave the nest." No longer coming home regularly, needing attention and care, they are now off and into a life of their own. And you are left with what's remaining in your life. If your husband is alive and your relationship is vital, there is much to experience. However, if the rest of life's social shelf is barren, your tears at your daughter's wedding will not be tears of joy.

For some women, the barren shelves make letting go very difficult. Eleanor, sixty, devoted her entire life to her three daughters. Under a constant barrage of criticism and berating by her resentful and hostile husband, she found meaning in her life as a homemaker. With her children grown, the now widowed Eleanor is facing acute Situational Loneliness. Instead of developing new relationships and exploring new interests, she copes with her loneliness through overinvolvement in her children's lives. Constantly worrying about them and punishing herself for past failures as a mother whenever she sees one of them unhappy, Eleanor is turning Situational Loneliness into Loneliness Out, because her children want to be free of her doting. Eleanor's life is in transition and Situational Loneliness needs to be dealt with by shifting gears rather than repairing the past.

Especially for men, stimulation bottoms out with loss of job, retirement, or illness. Herb, a career football coach who was successful enough to work at the professional level, was fired over a dispute with the management when he was fifty-five. He dealt with his job loss through denial. Instead of exploring other football-related employment, he kept meticulous up-to-date records of each team he used to coach against, as if he were preparing to play one of them that very weekend.

Not all men respond to job loss as bizarrely as Herb did. Some will experience depression and quiet anger. The sense of pain they feel makes it difficult for them to share their feelings with their families, and so there are protracted stretches of Situational Loneliness. Others may even experience sexual impotency. For many men, their job is what certifies their manhood. To lose one's job then becomes a castrating experience. Again, feelings are hidden and Situational Loneliness emerges.

Retirement is terrifying to many men. Nathan, in his late seventies, continues to work at his government job as well as at his consulting practice. Though he claims he keeps working because he needs the money to keep his family going, the evidence suggests that for Nathan, work and work relationships give his life purpose and meaning. Letting go of work would be letting go of life.

Indeed, men often die shortly after retiring. Little wonder in view of the psychological importance of work. When retirement means permanent separation from an activity which gives life much of its value—without a suitable substitute, the reason for staying alive may be called into question.

Serious illness is even more problematic. Louis was an aggressive lawyer. In his middle fifties, he suffered a severe skiing accident and incurred brain damage sufficient to impair some of his alertness and efficiency. Though able to discharge many of his duties, Louis found his new limitations so maddening, he gave up and entered a nursing home. He became so depressed, he cut off relations with his wife and children and lived a hermit's existence of extreme loneliness.

For Louis and others like him, serious illness or impairment means decreased productivity and sometimes a sense of diminished masculinity. As lifelong producers, men like Louis may no longer feel like men and may even question their right to live. It is for that reason that men who suffer long sieges of terminal illness experience such despair. More than the fear of death, they must confront the emotional debilitation arising from having to be dependent and passive rather than active and creative.

These trouble spots serve to reemphasize the importance of developing a firm identity and clear set of personal values such that life's meaning goes deeper than one's work. People who have profound social, spiritual, and moral values—who see themselves as children of God who are here for a reason—are less likely to turn Situational Loneliness into more severe forms of loneliness and depression.

LOSS OF FAMILIARITY

Situational Loneliness can also set in over a loss of familiarity. Moving out of a comfortable environment, changing jobs, entering the military, or going off to college means a break from the familiar and hence the secure, and a venture into the unknown.

Our preference for familiarity should not be underestimated. It shows in little ways in business and social groups. For example, college students, after one week of classes, will sit not only in the same row, but often in the same chair for the duration of the term. Somehow, that physical space becomes a mini-home to them. They feel secure there.

The unfamiliar is a source of Situational Loneliness because the usual reinforcements—rewards—are not there. In familiar surroundings, our own reality—our identity—is affirmed. People say hello, reminding us of our significance in their lives; our home is filled with evidence of our existence; our jobs, whether at home, office, or factory, point out what contribution we make to others and to the society at large. Stripped of these familiar markings, it is easy to feel insignificant, unimportant, and valueless. This is the same sensation of insignificance we feel walking down a city street that is teeming with scurrying people. These throngs of hurried people are a reminder not only of how many other humans there are, but also of how few know or care that we exist. We become a body—an object—for someone to get around, or a voice for a frazzled sales clerk to respond to curtly. Personhood is lost and Situational Loneliness sets in.

Mark, seventeen, is an agoraphobic. Whenever he has to travel a sizable distance from home—whether by car, bus, or train—he becomes nauseated and extremely ill. Though he loved basketball, he did not join the team because of the nausea he experienced on the bus trips to games at rival schools. As with so many agoraphobics, his condition gradually intensified. Mark was responding dramatically to any loss of familiarity. Somehow the unfamiliar was frightening, threatening. The more agoraphobic he became, the less of the unfamiliar he could endure, until he became a self-induced hostage in his own home. In Mark's case, it became so severe he was unable to go to school and had to be hospitalized.

For Mark, the answer was desensitization. Beginning with what little venturing out he could do, he built on that until going out became a challenge. He would try to outdo himself each time; and instead of avoiding the anxiety and nausea, he tried to relax in it and live through it, until it no longer held oppressive, fearful control over him.

In reality, Mark's problem was an extreme form of Situational Loneliness. He simply overreacted to situations which most people find problematic: dealing with the unfamiliar. Interestingly, Mark was also spiritually lonely. Highly religious and serious, he had developed a God-as-Chief-of-Police image. Hence, he was regularly ill at ease so that any additional lack of security set him off. The more he was able to revise his concept of God toward a more loving, merciful being, the less agoraphobic he became.

ROLE CHANGE

Situational Loneliness arising from unfamiliarity occurs whenever our roles change. Getting married ushers us into the world of the exciting, but unfamiliar and unexpected. As certain as you have gained a spouse, you have lost some of the familiar routines of single life. As a result, there are often pockets of loneliness, feelings of being adrift on an unfamiliar ocean.

Moreover, although your marriage will bring new friendships and acquaintances, it will end or alter others. There is a feeling of loss associated with relationships which will never again be, or at least will never be the same. It is a lonely and painful feeling.

Shifting into the role of parents may also trigger Situational Loneliness. As exciting and challenging as parenthood can be, it changes your relationship with your spouse, leaving you less time to be together. Sometimes you grow more toward your children and less toward your partner. Again, loss is felt, coupled with the sense of being in a strange though potentially rewarding situation.

Elizabeth, fifty, experienced a related type of loneliness. Having had a troubled, neglected childhood, she plodded through much of her parental role mechanically. Her husband, Phil, however, seemed to enjoy the children. Though quiet and unexpressive, he found being a parent satisfying responsibility and opportunity. For Elizabeth, this was difficult. She came to resent the attention Phil gave the children. She longed for him to care for her—to compensate for the deficits she had experienced as a child. Unable to communicate, Elizabeth and Phil found their marriage worsening until they separated, planning to divorce.

Just prior to the signing of the divorce agreement, Phil requested a reconciliation. Elizabeth was stunned and confused. After sorting through her feelings, it became clear that although Elizabeth dearly wanted a successful marriage with Phil, one of the critical issues for her was whether Phil was returning primarily because he missed the children.

Divorce will almost invariably bring on Situational Loneliness. Beyond the obvious Loneliness Out emanating from a lost marital relationship, there are other more immediate though temporary snags. When you get a divorce, you don't just divorce your spouse. Often you are divorcing your in-laws, friends gained through your marriage, organizations you joined, your community, and perhaps even your church. All of these are losses and all of them need to be grieved over to some extent. The grief is a form of Situational Loneliness—estrangement and deprivation that need to be seen through—experienced and acknowledged.

Beyond these losses, there is again an entrance into the unfamiliar single world. However, you are not just single again. You are a divorced person, coping with all that that label may imply. There is frequently fear and anxiety about facing the world so unprepared, so much alone.

Similar to divorce is *widowhood*. Here you had no choice in entering the new role. Nonetheless, you go through all the losses associated with divorce, but with the much more powerful and final impact of death. There is now no earthly opportunity to talk again with the lost spouse, no chance of human—not to mention marital—reunion.

Some try to escape their Situational Loneliness by denying reality. Although Leah, sixty-five, lost her husband several years ago, she has not admitted it even to herself. She lives alone, surrounded by memories of her departed spouse. In bed at night, she talks to her husband as if he were there next to her. Unable to sleep well, she listens to the radio and frequently phones call-in shows. Every time she calls in to my program, I know—regardless of the topic we are dealing with—that she will jaunt off into a pathetic series of reminiscences about the joyous relationship she had with her husband.

Tragically, by trying to summon her husband back from death, Leah is only intensifying her loneliness. Her children tire of being subjected to her ventures into unreality while her circle of friends continues to dwindle. Working through her Situational Loneliness, rather than denying its validity, and hence bringing on Loneliness Out, is the only answer for Leah.

Returning to the occupational arena, change of job means more than a shift in responsibilities. There is loneliness in the disruption and often loss of previous work relationships. There is also the ambiguity of dealing with new people and unfamiliar demands. Small patches of Situational Loneliness result. The fatigue and slight depression you feel after a job change is normal.

For many women, the major change is in the definition of the role of woman. The shift in the woman's role from one of homemaker, wife, and mother, to one encompassing a myriad of other life options is a dramatic one. Along with the excitement associated with more choices on the buffet of life options comes a confusion of not knowing what to select, along with a confrontation with the unfamiliar. However oppressive the traditional woman's role may have seemed for some, it was one with which many women were familiar and therefore comfortable in.

For women who encounter this changing role in mid-life, there is often more difficulty. On one hand, they may desire to sample new opportunities, due to their own inclinations as well as pressure from peers. Thus they may move beyond the homemaker role into the wider arena of a career or advanced education. Conflict, however subtle, arising from peer pressure, can have an alienating quality generating Situational Loneliness. On the other hand, making changes can disrupt family relationships. Your husband, who had become familiar with the traditional role, may be particularly resistant. Feeling the roles are being changed in the middle of the game, he may be hurt and angry. Either way, there is the prospect of Situational Loneliness, and a doublebind, can't-win situation may develop.

For women with a growing feminist consciousness, it is easy to become bitter over the unfairness of it all. For men have historically been able to sample an explosion of work opportunities and career alternatives without risking family disruption or loss. Women, however, are not granted such a waiver.

FEAR

In reality, the problem for most people is not Situational Loneliness. It is the fear of Situational Loneliness. Situational Loneliness (the lowest order of loneliness) itself is a normal, but unpleasant aspect of being alive—like getting up early in the morning. However, it becomes a psychological problem when it is feared. Situational Loneliness then becomes a threatening enemy—almost having a life of its own. It is the difference between finding Situational Loneliness unpleasant and experiencing it as traumatizing. The more you fear Situational Loneliness, the more you need to face it. You can never fully enjoy the stimulation of others' company if you are afraid of losing it. Under such conditions, you are always under threat, always living with the terror of abandonment.

Olivia's childhood was one long series of rejections and abandonment. Consequently, she grew up doubting that anyone would ever like her. Now, in her middle years, she still lives in such fear of losing a relationship, she refuses to be herself, believing that if she is, others will reject her. Not only do Olivia's problems rob her relationships of any genuine intimacy, they confine her in a prison of fear.

It is important to remind yourself that loneliness will not kill you. Painful and undesirable as it is, it will not destroy you. Dealing with Situational Loneliness is important because it is a test of how you will handle more intense and protracted forms of loneliness. You pass the test if you don't try to handle Situational Loneliness with the impulsivity of an adolescent—frantically trying to recruit people to fill the painful gaps. This is not to say that whenever you feel lonely and miss others, you should avoid them. It is to warn you not to become a "people junkie" so that you fly into a panic-driven state, scavenging your environment for human company whenever you feel unhappy and alone.

If Situational Loneliness triggers off deep insecurities, a sudden and acute feeling of abandonment (that "motherless child" sensation), it is a sign that you may need help in overcoming these irrational fears, sharpening your identity, and strengthening your self-esteem. Using some of the exercises discussed in earlier chapters is a good start. If you need therapeutic help, seek it. Remember, you will have to live the rest of your life with yourself—often alone—so it is wiser to build that self into the strongest and healthiest being possible: someone you can be comfortable with.

INTERNALS AND EXTERNALS

Dealing with Situational Loneliness touches the issue of the internal and external personality types discussed in chapter 5. An internal is one who takes total responsibility for his own feelings. When he is "down" he realizes he is not depressed because he is alone, unhappy because he is not getting enough respect, or angry because people put him down. Rather, he is aware that he is allowing himself to be depressed, unhappy, and angry by permitting the social environment to dictate his mood. He realizes that such "downer" states are brought on by his own irrational thinking and he will choose to change these moods by thinking differently and more rationally.

If an internal is depressed over Situational Loneliness, he may look at it as a form of either/or thinking. He reminds himself that loneliness is a part of being alive and that life is neither always lived with others nor always isolated. His depression is likely due to seeing life as totally lonely when he is alone or totally stimulating when he is with others. If he finds himself alone more than he wishes, he will examine his life to determine what he is doing to isolate himself.

He may find that he was minimaxing—minimizing or underestimating the amount of time he spends happily with others and by himself, while maximizing or overestimating the impact of the occasional lonely spots. He may also discover that he was employing glandular truth—letting momentary feelings dominate his entire view of reality; or even vacuum cleaning such that he was choosing to focus entirely on the unfulfilling aspects of life and so driving himself into a state of extreme unhappiness or depression.

Regardless, an internal sees that the negative feelings are in him. He has chosen to think himself into that state. Moreover, he realizes that he has the power to change—to think his way out of his dilemma. He can choose to think and therefore to feel differently.

Of course, internals do experience unhappiness and negative feelings. It is part of being human. But they accept those feelings as their own, not as caused by others who *make* them feel that way. As such, they rarely experience intense depression because they realize they can choose to think and feel differently if they make the effort.

The external is one who attributes his unhappiness to environmental forces. His spouse, children, job—whatever —*make* him feel that way. As such, he is setting himself up to be an emotional victim of any lonely situation because he has chosen to believe that the environment is the cause of his loneliness.

If you choose to think that way, you are choosing to be a victim, because there is a good deal of the environment which you cannot control. Friends move, spouses die, relationships end, children grow up, jobs disappear, and communities change... whether you like it or not. What you can control is how you are going to deal with those environmental realities—how you are going to approach those less than desirable events mentally. How you are going to think. Whether you are going to master your environment psychologically or whether you are going to let it master you. Externals deal with Situational Loneliness by trying to change the environment. They will call someone, go on a shopping spree, "pig out" on food, get drunk, or even take drugs in order to escape the loneliness. They will do everything but face it head-on.

Often, like Richard, they will withdraw. He had been seeing a young women—and, like Olivia, had great difficulty enjoying the relationship because he lived in constant fear of losing it. One day he told me of his apprehension over his friend's announced desire to come to his apartment that evening to talk.

"Why?" I asked.

"Well, she never does this. She never just says she wants to see me to talk about something important," he explained.

"But what is so threatening about it?" I asked again.

"I'm afraid she'll want to end the relationship," Richard confessed.

"What will you do if that's her decision?" I probed.

"I'm going to be so depressed.... I am just going to go under," he allowed self-pityingly.

"All right, you won't like it. So what will you do? Go out, get something to eat, and fight that feeling?" I asked, challenging his tendency to deal with it passively.

"Nah," Richard mumbled, "I'll just crawl into bed and try to sleep."

Richard is a classic external. He had decided to allow this young woman to determine how he was going to feel. And if the verdict she rendered was negative, Richard had already chosen to bury himself in a first-class depression.

But Richard doesn't see it that way. He feels that his depressions are chemically induced or are simply normal reactions to his crummy environment. Things just make him feel that way.

As an external, Richard feels he needs rather than wants a relationship. A relationship is not something that adds to the quality of his life; it *makes* his life. In fact, Richard lives with his aged mother because he "can't survive without her."

Instead of choosing to live his life at an even keel—in a healthy state of equilibrium—with meaningful relationships adding to the quality of an already involved life (see Figure 3a), Richard feels his life is utterly devoid of value. Hence, a relationship—particularly with a woman—is necessary to remove all that despair and make life worth living (Figure 3b).

Internals are typified by Figure 3a. They take the long view, realizing that they are responsible for what they think and how they behave. They tend to have a mature, stable perspective on life. Situational Loneliness, though never pleasant, is regarded by them as temporary, and life does go on even though other significant people may be gone. They do not see themselves as one of life's victims. They choose not to think and so not to feel this way.

They do not need people around constantly to affirm them, to help them feel good about themselves. They realize their own worth is a fixed determinant. Believers who are internals remind themselves that they are children of God, made in his image with a purpose for their existence, whether or not they are presently in a relationship. Though relationships can add to their life, they know there is nothing to fear about being alone.

Jerry learned this the hard way. After moving to a new

city, his marriage crumbled and his wife left him, taking their two children with her. About a year later, during an intense conversation, Jerry explained to me why he was doing so well, despite his less than ideal family situation.

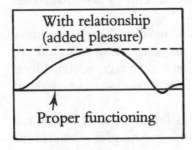

Figure 3a.

Figure 3b.

Note: The healthy person begins without a relationship and functions properly. With relationship, he goes above proper functioning. After loss, he dips below with broken heart syndrome, but only briefly; he then returns to proper functioning.

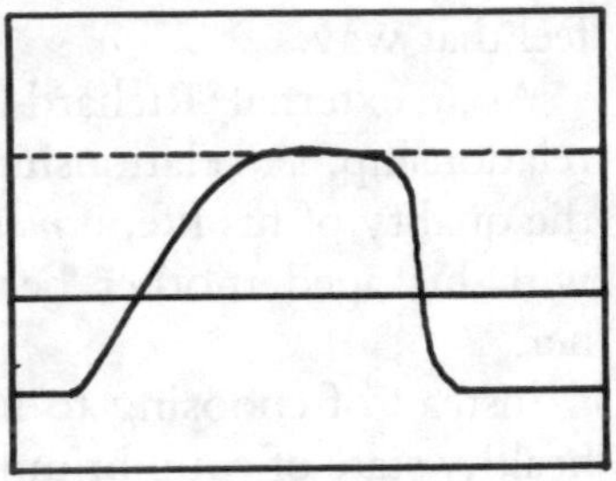

Note: This is the self-defeating pattern of being depressed without a relationship and then becoming manic (inappropriately high) with one, only to crash again when it ends.

"I went into counseling," he said, "and my therapist pointed out that human relationships don't determine life. They are not life itself. I began to realize that I had to carve out my own life, be more independent and responsible for how I felt; and then if a relationship came along I could enjoy it as an added bonus. All this time, I had desperately tried to hold my marriage together because I was afraid of being all but dead without Pam. I can honestly tell you I now feel better than I ever have, even though I do have to deal with some loneliness."

If anything, Situational Loneliness reminds us that we are

all, in the last analysis, external, in that we are utterly dependent on God. We realize in our loneliness that we really can count on nothing and no one other than God to pull us through. People will and do regularly disappoint us. Even when we are with them, there is often Loneliness In due to boredom, fights, or alienation. Everything around us changes and the pace of change is intensifying. The only unchanging relationships available are those with God and ourselves.

For externals, Situational Loneliness is frightening, often because it means a confrontation with self. Often fear and guilt emerge as you peer into yourself. If you don't like yourself; feel a vague but pervasive sense of guilt; or tend to rely on others to entertain, cheer you up, or in other ways take care of you—then being alone is threatening. When alone, instead of being able to escape from loneliness by looking in the face of others and hearing their voices, you have to look into life's mirror, seeing and hearing yourself as you really are.

This was the problem for Tara, mentioned earlier. Raised by an abusive father, she came to see herself as worthy only of others' anger. Self-hate and feelings of inner isolation calcified, such that she would lash out at others whenever she sniffed the slightest scent of being disliked. She fractured one relationship after another this way. However, as painful as those confrontations were, being alone was even more devastating for Tara because it left her alone with the one person she hated most: herself. So Tara hopped from one friend to another, one family member to another, one lover to another—hoping that somewhere and from someone she would be able to extract the good feelings about herself which would eradicate the irrational and destructive messages she had internalized from her now dead father.

For Tara, Situational Loneliness was best handled by being alone. Patient but persistent counseling, along with self-examination, is what was necessary for Tara to rethink and so revise her feelings about herself. A positive self-image and a greater sense of emotional maturity is not something that can be obtained by chasing after others who hold "the key to the candy store" of positive affirmation. Self-confidence is developed and nurtured through independent effort.

WHAT TO DO

The first thing to keep in mind when Situational Loneliness hits, is that it is just that: situational. It is temporary; it will pass. This awareness undercuts much of the power of the experience. The temptation toward impulsive, frightened behavior is lessened.

It is also important to remind yourself again that it is a normal part of life. Whether your Situational Loneliness is the result of moving to a new neighborhood, being away from your family on a trip, or even losing a loved one, the sensation of Situational Loneliness is universal. Everyone experiences it. The only unique thing about it is that you are the only one you know who is feeling it now. Reminding yourself of the universality of loneliness reduces its pain because you know that even though you may not be in their company, you are in harmony with a large number of people. As such, you realize that not only are there others who feel lonely, but there are others who can understand exactly how you feel.

Despite your awareness of its common and temporary nature, it is important to do something about your Situational Loneliness. Pulling the covers over your head like Richard is not the answer. However, rummaging through your address book in a frenzy, hoping to find someone to dump your loneliness on is no answer either. Rational action is the key.

Being rational means not being afraid of loneliness. If you feel a sense of fear or panic, repeat to yourself three times, "I can take care of myself." This auto-suggestion sows in your mind the seeds of internal thinking; you can lower the level of threat you experience, no longer feeling your psychological survival is at stake.

You may be tempted to dismiss this exercise, realizing rationally that you will not die from Situational Loneliness. However, that is just the problem. When you are panicking, you are not handling it rationally. The experience is not being processed realistically. This exercise will help return the dial on your psychological stove from "irrational high" to "rational pilot."

In any case, don't be afraid of it. Situational (or for that matter, any other type of loneliness) is not an animal which attacks you. It is a form of inner psychological pain, and instead of wallowing in self-pity, or being driven into a frenzy, the best question you can ask when it arrives is, "What am I going to do about it?"

Any time you can anticipate Situational Loneliness—knowing you are going to move, face a separation, or in some other way experience unpleasant isolation—one thing you can do is plan for it. Too often, people face the enemy of Situational Loneliness unarmed. Although they know they will have to confront it, they do not prepare for it. Preparing for Situational Loneliness reminds them of its inevitable reality; so they deny it, as if, by avoiding it, Situational Loneliness will go away.

An important part of the planning process is to determine what your interests, hobbies, and favorite projects are—those which are social and those which are solitary. Then bring into your plan some people-centered activities you enjoy, as well as the solitude you need to grow in the inner person.

Mel modeled effective planning with regard to his retirement. Several years before, he began developing a series of nonoccupational interests in projects—ranging from woodworking to visiting friends, taking leadership roles in organizations to reading. He increased his involvement in these activities as retirement approached. He managed to cultivate such an intense interest in these pursuits, he began looking forward to spending more time with them. So, when retirement day came, Mel was ready. The transition was smooth and pleasant. His retirement party was a joy rather than a cruel reminder that his days as an employee were over. Consequently, Mel exemplified the cliché of being busier after he retired than when he was employed.

In any case, planning for Situational Loneliness—whether it be for a brief period such as when you are on a trip, or something longer as in the case of moving away—should include both active and passive stimulation. Visiting people, participating in group events, and getting out into other activity-laden experiences need to be balanced off against solitude, reading, watching television, etc. An even rhythm is important in retaining your rational equilibrium. Moreover, examine yourself, determining whether you tend to be a Tara or a Richard—a people junkie who frantically tries to fill the void with human company; or someone who simply pulls life's covers over his head, trying to withdraw. If you lean in either direction, plan your Situational Loneliness agenda to compensate for that tendency.

If you don't anticipate any imminent Situational Loneliness, having a plan is no less important, because sooner or later the need will most certainly arise. Even if you believe you never experience loneliness, upon closer look, you will probably discover that your life contains occasional, though brief, lonely periods. Analyze how well you handle them and plan accordingly. Regardless, having a battle plan ready to confront Situational Loneliness is especially helpful for those who rarely face it. They need particular help in reducing the panic and easing the pain of something with which they have limited experience.

Any time Situational Loneliness is suddenly thrust upon you, there are several immediate steps you can take. Begin by sitting down and thinking through your situation as rationally as possible. Repeat the, I-can-take-care-of-myself statement to yourself as often as necessary to retain control.

174

Once you have reestablished your rationality, you have removed the biggest barrier to successful functioning.

Another effective immediate step is to find every familiar element you can in your environment. For example, if you are in another country, determine how to find other English-speaking people. If you are in a strange city, you could locate people who have religious, political, or social interests similar to yours. If you are widowed, reach out to others who know you and have dealt successfully with this tragic predicament. Such action will affirm your own reality and sense of significance.

Also, to whatever extent possible, organize your environment. After moving into a new home, try to gain psychological control by putting things away in their proper places. If you are in a hotel, hang up your clothes and put your personal items where you want them, making the room as homey as possible. In short, attempt to master as much of your environment as necessary. This cuts the threat of the unfamiliar and unknown down to size.

Most important, even though you know the Situational Loneliness is temporary, take rational action. Take control of your circumstances. Use your plan. Do not wait the loneliness out or overreact by careening from person to person. If you do seek out the company of others, it is helpful to review the people-meeting skills discussed in chapter 4.

If, after developing a plan and rehearsing the immediate steps for encountering Situational Loneliness, you still sense a gnawing fear of it, desensitize yourself by *choosing* some Situational Loneliness. Voluntarily put yourself through tests by purposely isolating yourself for set periods of time, evaluating how you handle being alone. Perhaps you can begin by retreating to total isolation, say for a few hours every Thursday afternoon or evening. In this case, use only passive, no-human-contact stimulation to deal with the loneliness. This means no company, not answering the phone, nothing. Once you can handle such planned brief periods, extend the time to an entire afternoon or evening.

Although this voluntary method is not a perfect replica of genuine Situational Loneliness, because familiar people are available to you, it is highly effective because it develops your ability to be alone. Moreover, it becomes a very realistic practice when you are feeling that you don't want to be alone on a scheduled day, yet you force yourself to go through with it. In any case, you will have proven to yourself conclusively that you can take care of yourself, and that awareness will shortcircuit the panic associated with the, "Oh, no! I'm alone now!" feeling.

Indeed, there is nothing to fear. Loneliness is a normal part of life. You can handle it. You can be liberated from loneliness.

8

QUESTIONS
AND ANSWERS

Following are the responses to some of the most common questions people have about loneliness and related issues. The questions are based on my radio, research, speaking, teaching, and personal life experiences.

Are self-help books ever effective?
The biggest problem I have with many self-help books is that, despite their how-to claims, they really offer no concrete instructions. They discuss and hash out problems in insightful detail, but the reader is left with no real direction in dealing with them. They give diagnosis without prescription.

However, if a book does offer clear direction, it will do the reader no good unless he applies the prescriptions to his own life. Too many readers go through such books, feeling excited over how sensitively the author diagnoses and prescribes for the problem, then fail to follow any of the author's advice. I believe that if readers really employed the suggestions contained in the better self-help books, they would get results.

Why do you say that loneliness is the number one psychological problem of our time?

It is the number one *perceived* problem. It is the problem people are most acutely aware of; the one they experience consciously. There is much evidence of how greatly people fear loneliness. For those experiencing Loneliness Out, the popularity of everything from singles' bars to dating services attests to people's desire not to be alone.

Moreover, often people will remain in extremely hurtful relationships simply because they don't want to face the alternative: being alone. Thus they will avoid confronting critical issues in marriage, romance, and friendship out of fear that the confrontation could bring dissolution.

In marriage, this fear of being alone can be so intense that couples who argue frequently, have nothing in common, and are apart a great deal of the time will still feel safer at home, just knowing their partner is in the next room— even if they don't see him all night.

Although loneliness has always been a problem (as suggested in chapter 1), today we live in a society which intensifies it greatly. On one hand, we see and deal with more people than ever; on the other, we deal with them *briefly*—superficially. As a result, it feels as if we are dining on insubstantial, social junk food. Sometimes we can get a social fill quickly, but it doesn't last long. We have quantity without quality.

In addition, many of us are far away—both in distance and life style—from our social origins. We are separated from our roots and are regularly coping with the unfamiliar. With the average family moving once every five years, the process of breaking away from the familiar and entering the unknown is regularly repeated. Furthermore, often we marry someone from a background much different from our own. Therefore, our spouses cannot reinforce the roots of our identity. And if we do live at great distance from our original families, it is tempting to place even greater pressure than ever on our marriage partner to meet our desire for intimacy.

All these factors contribute to a pervasive loneliness. Though we get much practice in social skills which help us deal with people on the surface, there is a lack of opportunity to relate to others in depth. And this makes it difficult to practice meaningful relational skills—which, in turn, makes it more difficult for our relationships to work.

Why is loneliness so painful?
When we enter the world, we are with others. Our mother takes care of us and so we learn to be dependent right from the start. Others teach us what love, care, and human worth are all about. We must internalize that love and worth so that we can become independent, feeling good about ourselves under any circumstance. If not, being alone brings with it feelings of fear, abandonment, and betrayal— the feeling that no one wants or needs you, and therefore that you are of no value. You feel you are in the world for no purpose and with no meaning. If hell is total separation from God, then its earthly counterpart has to be the feeling that we are totally separated—not just alone, but cut off— from human care and meaning. For this reason, it is so important to develop and internalize feelings of self-worth. Then we can be more independent, carrying those good feelings around inside of us whether or not we are in a relationship.

Which type of loneliness is the worst?
It depends on the individual. Some people feel less pain and "better" with one type of loneliness than another. What we can say is that Situational Loneliness is the least problematic because it is intermittent and temporary (though it can be argued that any type of Situational Loneliness falls under one of the other four categories).

However, if pressed on the matter, I would say Intrapsychic Loneliness is the worst because it suggests that you are not clear about who you are. If your identity and values are defined, it is much easier to deal with any other type of loneliness.

I would think Loneliness Out is the worst. That's the one most people complain about.
There is no doubt that Loneliness Out is difficult. (A good deal of this book focuses on it.) However, if you can overcome Intrapsychic and Spiritual Loneliness, you have laid the foundation for handling Loneliness Out effectively. You may have some things left to learn in dealing with Loneliness Out, but you have the psychological tools to do so.

Which type of loneliness requires the most work?
Intrapsychic Loneliness and Spiritual Loneliness, because each of these is the result of the way we have been taught to see ourselves and God, usually in the beginning years of life. Anything learned that early tends to be resistant to change. Not only has it been with us very long and so is foundational to how we look at life, but we learned it before we were old enough to question it.

Are people usually lonely in more than one way?
Yes. Although it is easy to separate the various types of loneliness on paper for purposes of analysis and explanation, they do overlap. Of course, overcoming one type of loneliness can make dealing with others less difficult.

Are certain people more prone to loneliness than others?
We need to separate loneliness from being alone. Indeed, externals will likely experience more loneliness than internals, regardless of how little or much they are alone.

Moreover, middle class people who are constantly busy and active are often high risks because they spend so little time being alone and without things to do. Their limited experience with solitude can render them vulnerable to intense bouts with loneliness. Certainly, lower income people confront much loneliness. My therapy experience in working with them affirms that. However, often they are emotionally tougher because their experience with day-to-day survival living has a toughening effect. As a result, they often tend to fear loneliness less, though finding it no more pleasant than anyone else.

Can you be vulnerable to loneliness and not know it?
As mentioned previously, if your life is packed with people and stimulating experiences so that you never have to spend time on "hold," you may feel very strong and in control emotionally. However, once the stimulation machine shuts off, you may be in for a painful experience because you are faced with an enemy you have not been prepared to deal with.

Are people who are lonely mentally ill?
Except for severe cases such as certain forms of what are termed psychoses, I don't believe people with emotional problems are mentally ill. I don't believe that they have brain damage. Rather, I believe that people experience problems in living and these problems owe to distorted perceptions of life.

Loneliness itself is normal and doesn't imply any severe psychological problem. The question is whether a person can master loneliness or is defeated by it.

Why do people get anxiety attacks when they feel lonely?
There is no such thing as an anxiety attack. Anxiety is not a nasty, furry animal which leaps out at you from the outside. It is an inner mental episode. People usually experience anxiety episodes because they think frightening, "Here I am, abandoned and unloved!" thoughts with which they drive themselves into a frenzy.

The best thing to do if you experience these episodes is

to realize it; and when you feel one coming, don't fight it, but instead let the anxiety flow through you, reminding yourself that it will pass and you will not die from it. Once you stop fearing anxiety, the experience loses its power and becomes less frequent.

What is the relationship between loneliness and depression?
Loneliness is a normal, though unpleasant state. Depression results from a feeling of hopelessness. If you let loneliness get you down, feeling it will never end, and that there is no reason to be happy, you can turn loneliness into depression.

You speak of proper functioning. What do you mean?
I define six levels of psychological functioning:
(A) displaced: autistic, self-contained, split from reality;
(B) frozen: depressed, lonely, intimidated, passive;
(C) defending: responding, reacting to the environment either actively and aggressively or passively and conformingly; (D) functioning: coping, existing, lacking in spontaneity; (E) venturing: exploring, risk-taking, experimenting; (F) total living: invested, choosing and shaping, living with emotional maturity.

As you can see, these levels range all the way from what lay people would term insanity to optimum functioning. Loneliness falls into the frozen level. Obviously, the goal is to overcome it and move up to total living.

You mention therapy a great deal. What is it and how does one pick the right therapist?
There are two questions here. First, therapy is a process aimed at helping you reduce confusion and emotional pain, while enabling you to function effectively individually and socially. Often, psychological problems—whether they be depression, self-hate, insecurity, or intense anxiety—owe to thought distortions (something we discuss in the book). A therapist acts as an experienced, objective force to help

you dispel those distortions and return you to proper living.

However, a therapist does not solve your problems. He helps *you* solve them. This is a primary reason why some people benefit from therapy and others don't. Some want to learn and grow, and will work at it; others are looking for someone to *make* them better.

There is no magic formula for picking a good therapist. I believe the two criteria for a good therapist are to find someone you have confidence in and feel comfortable with. Confidence is vital, because without it you will not be able to drop your resistance and work out your problems. Feeling comfortable is perhaps even more important because if you don't like your therapist, you will not be open with him and little progress will be made.

Let me add a few other points. Proper training does not guarantee a therapist will be good. For example, there are psychiatrists who are terrible; and ministers, trained in pastoral counseling, who are excellent. Your therapist may be a psychiatrist, psychologist, psychiatric social worker, clergyman (schooled in pastoral counseling), or someone else. The key is what skills he or she has and whether you feel the person is right for you.

Moreover, don't be taken in by the myth that you get what you pay for. There are therapists who charge $80 per hour and will do you no good; while others may operate on a sliding pay-as-you-can scale and are excellent.

If you want to enter therapy, inquire as to who is reputed to be good. Then make an initial appointment. Tell the therapist what you are troubled by and see how you feel with him.

Above all, don't try to be "superman" or "superwoman" and try to go it alone because you think therapy is for wimps. It takes a great deal more courage to open up and face your problems than to try to avoid them—hiding under a facade of seeming "together." In the long run, it is a lot more rewarding, too.

How do you know if you need therapy?
Life is difficult. Once you accept that reality, rather than
chase the psychological equivalent of the silver chalice, you
are on your way to solving many of your problems. The
question is whether or not the difficulties in your life are
being experienced as overwhelming, and as such are
impairing your ability to function in your day-to-day life;
or whether you can accept them as part of being alive and
deal with them effectively.

*You talk about the importance of faith in being a healthy person.
How do you answer the charge that Christianity is a crutch?*
Christianity *is* a crutch. However, it is a necessary one
because we need crutches. We are all flawed, mortal beings;
none of us is going to get out of this world alive. The issue
then is not whether Christianity is a crutch, but whether it
is a valid one.

Everyone uses some crutch. It may be subtle and
psychological—pride, defensiveness, dependency on other
people—or more obvious, such as alcohol, drugs, materialism, or sex. Unfortunately, these are rubber crutches.
In the final analysis, they will not support us. Faith in
Christ will.

*What is the main reason why it is so tempting to use self-defeating
methods like food, alcohol, sex, etc., to deal with loneliness?*
Because they bring instant relief even though they provide
no long-term solution. When we are suffering, we tend to
be very vulnerable to anything which will relieve pain,
regardless of whether it helps us.

Also, it is easier to escape a problem than to work
through it. The tragedy is that the self-defeating alternatives
ultimately leave us with two problems: our loneliness and
a self-defeating habit we need to break.

*Does the reported increase in sexual activity outside of marriage
correlate with growing levels of loneliness in this society?*

I think so. Sex is the closest we can get to someone else physically. It seems logical that when people feel alone emotionally, they will be more vulnerable to bridge that gap impulsively by becoming sexually involved. This is especially true for people who have difficulty forming healthy relationships. Sex does not require talking—having the courage to expose who you are as a person, as well as bodily. Moreover, in sex you can fantasize that what is going on is an exchange of love and personal intimacy, even if it is not.

The problem with much sexual activity is that rather than being a physical manifestation of the relational love and closeness two people have achieved, often it precedes relational intimacy. As such, it is unfulfilling and even emotionally painful. In addition, when it precedes, rather than reflects relational closeness, it drives people together physically who are unprepared to be together as persons. Often after sex, they feel frightened and confused, wondering, "What do we do now?"

What do you do if, out of feeling lonely and depressed, you develop a destructive, compulsive habit like overeating?
First off, such responses to loneliness are extremely common. Smoking, drinking, and eating tend to head the list of self-defeating response patterns. Among the many reasons for developing these habits is that we perceive them as signs of love and companionship amid our loneliness. In fact, for years, one cigarette company capitalized on this tendency with a jingle, "Me and my Winstons, we've got a real good thing." In short, the presence of cigarettes, alcohol, or food becomes a substitute for human company.

Begin dealing with these habits by facing them for what they are: self-defeating ways of coping with loneliness and a result of your own less than positive self-concept. Seeing such patterns for what they are is so vital that the first step to recovery among alcoholics attending Alcoholics Anonymous is to stand up publicly and proclaim, "I am an alcoholic." You need to stand up and admit to yourself and preferably to others, "I am hurting myself by using _____ as a substitute for people."

Once you really want to stop, *decide* to do so. That's right, realize that you have a choice in how you are going to treat yourself and decide to treat yourself properly. Then do what is necessary to overcome the pattern. If you need help, there are organizations, from AA to Smoking Clinics to Overeaters Anonymous, which can help you once you have taken the biggest first step: deciding you are going to stop.

Can a person be psychologically healthy without faith?
Yes, in the sense that people can function well if they have a clear sense of who they are, have a positive self-image, and a willingness to take responsibility for their own well-being. Though they may be using the crutch of pride and self-sufficiency to some extent, they may do quite well personally and socially.

The problem many such people do experience is the sense that something is missing. There is a void, a lack of inner fulfillment and certain purpose to life. However, this does not necessarily impair their ability to function well and experience much happiness.

Shouldn't believers experience less loneliness due to their relationship with God?
Ideally, yes. However, often our relationship with God is riddled with insecurities and hangups so that we have difficulty deriving sufficient peace from it. To paraphrase Scripture, if you have trouble relating to those you *can* see, how much more difficult it is to deal with one you cannot see. Although I certainly would not negate the healing effect of a relationship with God, I would emphasize that often we can use it as a cop-out for dealing with our own problems.

I remember Jean, a middle-aged woman, who lived

virtually incarcerated with her mother. Her mother used every available guilt-imputing device to keep Jean from going out and being on her own. So, Jean simply remained home, tended her mother, and stayed desperately lonely. When I asked her what she was going to do about breaking out and becoming an independent adult, Jean said, "I'm just leaving it in God's hands."

Though her theology was good, she was using it as an excuse to avoid facing up to her problem of being manipulated and imprisoned by her mother's guilt-dealing tactics.

Aren't you being insensitive when you say other people don't make us unhappy? It seems as if you don't expect people to be responsible for how they treat others, if others' feelings are their own problems.
On the contrary. You are responsible for your actions— regardless of how people feel about them. You are no less responsible for being cruel to others if they aren't troubled by it, then you would be if they are. Your responsibility ends, however, where their mind begins. You cannot change how they feel unless they want you to. As long as you think you cause other people's feelings and they cause yours, you are opening yourself to manipulating and being manipulated—blaming others and being blamed by them for feelings which are intensely personal.

You also seem to believe people are totally responsible for whether they are internal or external. Is that fair? Aren't some people brought up to be external and others internal?
In a human sense, life is not always fair. Indeed, some parents instill internal thinking patterns in their children, while others pound in external notions. However, once you are an adult and you realize what side of the ledger you're on, it is up to you to do something about it. Of course, it will be more difficult if you have been raised as an external. But no one is going to step in and change that for you. You must choose to do it.

What if you have a friend who, no matter what you do, remains very lonely and depressed? What can you do to cheer him up?
Nothing. You cannot make other people happy. If they choose to remain lonely and miserable, they have the right to do so. All the commiserating or cajoling in the world will not rouse them out of their state unless they want to get out. Once they truly want to break out, they can be helped.

If you are experiencing Loneliness In, what do you do if your partner refuses to deal with the issue of your poor relationship?
Again, there is nothing you can do. If you have related to him how you are feeling in a way which does not pin the blame for your unhappiness on him, it is up to him to respond. If he refuses to, determine what options you have left—demanding that he respond or you will separate, ending the relationship; or staying, while moving more toward developing your own life apart from the relationship. And make a choice. Whatever you do, take action. Just sitting there is a formula for turning loneliness into depression.

Is loneliness ever good?
To the extent that you can learn a great deal about life from it, it is not always a negative experience. Indeed, a person who has never dealt with loneliness is missing out on an important part of the human spectrum of experience. Moreover, it is difficult to appreciate the fullness and potential of human relationships unless you have faced off with the opposite. However, this does not make loneliness pleasant.

Don't relationships meet emotional needs?
There is no doubt that life can be more fulfilling and pleasant with certain things, such as meaningful relationships, in it. However, the danger lies in the word, "need." I remember a very clever, manipulative radio commercial

which encouraged listeners to borrow money for luxuries on the grounds that, "If we want something bad enough, it becomes a need."

Heresy! It becomes *perceived* as a need.

The key to life—in or out of relationships—is to be your own person, stop looking to others for approval, and don't feel sorry for yourself. No one will take care of you but yourself. When you do that, you can meet many of your own emotional wants, such that relationships only add to your life's fulfillment.

What then is the value of good relationships?
They are stimulating and invigorating, adding zest and intensity to life. Good relationships affirm (not determine or create) our identity and worth. Such affirmation almost always feels good. Relationships tell us that we are wanted and valued by others. Being wanted is also very rewarding.

In short, good relationships are wonderful. They have an enriching effect on healthy people. We need to appreciate their worth rather than depend on them for our own worth.

Can you be alone and happy?
None of us is really alone. Even if we are not involved in an intense relationship, usually we are surrounded by people, in addition to having a phone which can put us in contact with others. So, being alone is a matter of degree.

However, if you lack a meaningful relationship, you most certainly still can be happy. Begin by reminding yourself again that relationships add to life, they do not make life. Realize that the person who is in charge of your earthly happiness and the quality of your life is you—no one else can take control of your mind, cleansing it of external notions and thought distortions. Then, looking carefully at what aspects of life you can control and what you cannot, focus on the areas within your domain and move toward making your life happy.

Is there any kind of loneliness which is impossible to overcome?
No. Not if you are willing to take responsibility for your
own feelings and work at it.

*Are any of the methods you suggest in dealing with loneliness
foolproof?*
There are always individual differences involved. I suggest
a variety of exercises and techniques for each type of
loneliness so that individuals can pick the ones which are
most effective in liberating them, adapting them to their
personal use.

There is, however, one which never fails. That is taking
responsibility for your own emotional well-being. You can
never go wrong using that as your starting point.

A Handful of Suggested Responses to Loneliness

1. Get out the directory of a church or organization to which you belong. Phone the person who is listed below you.
2. Get out an organization's Zip Code directory. Figure out who lives closest to you and arrange to meet that person for coffee within a day or two.
3. Bake or buy something for your next-door neighbor.
4. Ask your spouse/roommate/child/neighbor to go for a walk.
5. Buy a roll of black and white film. Take pictures of neighborhood children.
6. Start cleaning a desk, file, or closet that contains old papers, photographs, yearbooks, etc. Get sidetracked reminiscing.
7. Go buy yourself two flowers; give one away.
8. Place a five-minute long distance call to a friend or relative.
9. Make definite plans for a week from Friday with at least two other people.
10. Jog around the block.
11. Sign up for a course.
12. Read aloud to someone.
13. Volunteer to help someone or an organization for a specified short period of time.
14. Write about your feelings. Keep a journal.
15. Don't fight it. Savor loneliness as proof of the universal need for God and others.

Carol Christian

For information on
Dr. David Claerbaut's seminars
on loneliness, write:

David Claerbaut and Associates
5061 North St. Louis
Chicago, IL 60625